THE
JOKIEST
JOKING TRIVIA
BOOK EVER
WRITTEN... NO JOKE!

THE
JOKIEST
JOKING TRIVIA
BOOK EVER
WRITTEN...NO JOKE!

1,001 SURPRISING FACTS TO AMAZE YOUR FRIENDS

by Brian Boone
Illustrations by Amanda Brack

CASTLE POINT BOOKS

NEW YORK

The Library of Congress Cataloging-in-Publication Data is available
upon request.

ISBN 978-1-250-19976-8 (trade paperback)
ISBN 978-1-250-19975-1 (ebook)

Our books may be purchased in bulk for promotional, educational, or
business use. Please contact your local bookseller or the Macmillan
Corporate and Premium Sales Department at 1-800-221-7945, extension
5442, or by email at MacmillanSpecialMarkets@macmillan.com.

First Edition: September 2018

10 9 8 7 6 5 4 3 2 1

To M. and B.

Fun fact: You're the best!

CONTENTS

From a bug to an airplane to a banana, everything is full of amazing, almost unbelievable details just waiting to be discovered. And we're excited to bring some of the zaniest facts to you and your friends.

So get ready to jump into 10 whole chapters—hundreds of pages worth—of strange facts, cool trivia, and eye-opening stories. For example . . .

- The man who wrote the Declaration of Independence *also* invented the swivel chair.

- Wombat poop is cube-shaped.

- Summer on the planet Uranus lasts for more than 20 years.

- The longest model railway in the world is 10 miles long.

- The biggest pumpkin ever grown was the size of a car.

- Plus lots, lots more wacky facts, jokey commentary, and hilarious illustrations!

We had so much fun putting this book together. The only problem was narrowing down all the great information we found to *only* 1,001 facts! (Maybe a sequel?)

Fun fact to get you started: You're going to have a blast reading (and sharing) these jokiest trivia bits!

1
BODY OF KNOWLEDGE

The human body is a complex system of organs, muscles, bones, and electric impulses . . . which means there's a lot of weird and cool stuff to learn about it.

Did you know that your butt deserves an award?
It wins first prize for being the biggest
muscle in your body!
They don't call it the *gluteus maximus* for nothing!

It takes a team of about **300 different muscles working together to get you to stand up** (and stay standing without falling flat on your face). *Blame* them *when you take a trip!*

Boom-boom, boom-boom . . .
Over the course of a lifetime, **your heart will beat somewhere around 2.5 billion times.**

There are exactly **206 bones in your body.** (We counted.) *More than half* of those are in your hands, fingers, feet, and toes.

Why do babies, puppies, and kittens catch our eye with their cuteness? Their eyes, which appear huge in their little bodies! Eyeballs actually stay the same size from birth.

A man grows an average of about 16½ feet of facial hair. Thankfully, it's not all at once but over the course of his life!

The reason your nose runs when you cry really hard: **Tears drain out of your eyes . . . and into your nose.** And then they come out your nose. *(With a bunch of other stuff.)*

Think how cold you are when you forget your winter coat. Now consider how cold you'd be without your *skin*. **Your skin weighs the same as *four* heavy winter coats.**

Technically, **urine is sterile and germ-free**.
But you definitely shouldn't drink it.

This fact stinks!
**In just its first week of life, a newborn baby
will go through 80 diapers.**

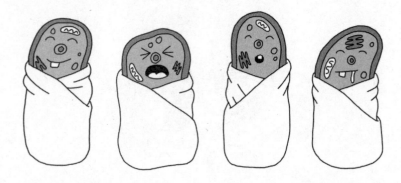

While you were reading that last fact, 30 million cells
in your body died. But millions of new cells will be
born in your body as you're reading the
rest of this book!

You've got a lot of growing up to do.
**At birth, your brain weighed 3 ounces.
As an adult, it'll weigh 3 pounds.**
All that knowledge weighs a lot!

**The hardest substance in your body
is the enamel on your teeth**, even though
it's one 1000th of an inch thick.
And that's the tooth!

Looking sharper every day!
Fingernails grow at a rate of about one 25th of an inch per week.

Every two weeks, your stomach produces a new layer of protective mucus.
If it didn't, it would digest itself.
Your stomach is its own worst enemy.

Hope you're hungry:
In your lifetime, you'll eat about 60,000 pounds of food.
That's the equivalent weight of six elephants.

"Fathead" isn't necessarily an insult.
The organ that contains the most fat is the brain.
It's about 60 percent fat!

McIntosh or Granny Smith scent?
They didn't have deodorant in 16th-century
England, so people put apple slices under
their armpits to absorb B.O.

What's the point?
The exact point where your nose meets your forehead
has a name. It's called the *nasion*.

**After being used for 10 years, a mattress
doubles in weight.**
Why? It gets loaded up with dust mites, mold,
dead skin cells, hair, and dried sweat.
Sweet dreams!

Hair grows incredibly slowly. **It takes 30 days for a human hair to grow just one half of an inch.**
You grow, hair!

Care for some mouthwash?
The average person's mouth is one of the most germ-infested places in the world. **There are more germs in a mouth than there are on a public toilet seat.**

Go ahead, act all cool...
A fist bump spreads just 10 percent of the
microbes that a full-on handshake does.

Cold comfort:
It's not the cold virus that makes you feel awful—it's your body fighting it off.
The immune system releases white blood cells to attack the virus and force it out, resulting in headaches and stuffy noses.

Sorry, sad astronauts:
If you cry in space, the tears don't roll down.
They stick to the face.

That's sick! **The stomach flu, a nasty virus that leads to vomiting and diarrhea, isn't really the flu.** It's actually *gastroenteritis.*

You'll never need eye mittens! **It's impossible for your eyes to freeze** even when it gets really cold. The salt in your tears prevents that from happening.

Don't call them "eye boogers."
That gunk that forms in your eyes
while you sleep is called *rheum*.

In your eyes, it's a fine line between love and hate.
**When you see someone you love, your pupils *dilate*,
or get larger.** They also get bigger when you're looking
at someone you *really don't like*.

**The white of your eye isn't technically called
the "white of your eye."** It's called the *sclera*.

Don't blink . . . or do.
You blink about 15 times a minute. Over a lifetime,
that's two years spent with your eyes shut!

That's a big box of crayons!
**The human eye can recognize 10 million
different colors.**
You may not even ever see them all.
You can't even count that fast.

**Your eyes move back and forth to take everything in
about 80 times a second.** That's about 4.6 million
times a day!

The vast majority of people have blue eyes or brown eyes.
Only 2 percent of the human population has green eyes.
Let's go green!

A blind man named Daniel Kish taught himself echolocation. He hikes and mountain bikes by listening for the echo of his tongue clicks. *Sounds amazing.*

Tears are made up primarily of water and salt. That means **tears are almost exactly the same thing as urine.** *Is that why people go to the bathroom when they need to cry?*

Taking in the skin you're in: **Every day, you inhale a lot of your own skin flakes.** About 700,000 of them, to be more exact.

Some sleep experts say one way to cure insomnia is to wear socks and mittens to bed. This little piggy went to sleep...

The thickest skin on your body is the stuff
on the bottom of your feet. It's three times thicker
than the skin on the palm of your hands.
And that's no small feet!

Got a blister, mister?
If it's a big one, it's called a *vesicle*.
If it's a small one, that's a *bullae*.

Does something about this seem fishy?
There's a rare condition called *ichthyosis*
that makes human skin appear scaly.

Get thee to a doctor!
**In Medieval England, freckles were called
"moth-patches."**
They were considered a serious health problem.

Do you dream in color? Apparently only 5 percent
of Americans do, with the rest dreaming in
black and white.
Either way, we all dream in "weird."

Don't I know you from somewhere?
**Your brain doesn't invent new faces for people
in your dreams.** They're all faces you've seen
before—say, strangers on the street or people on TV.

Sleep like a grownup . . .
The average adult has four dreams a night.
They only have about one really bad nightmare a year.

Ever start talking and suddenly just blank out, or "have a brain fart"? That's what's called a maladaptive brain activity change. Only a slightly less embarrassing kind of fart.

If it takes you less than five minutes to fall asleep, that means you're sleep-deprived. Healthy sleepers need about 10 to 15 minutes to head off to Sleepyland. *The sheep are counting!*

Hair it is!
Even if you don't have a lot of hair, your body is still naturally cycling out old ones for new ones. **You lose about 50 to 100 hairs a day.**

Imagine wanting green teeth . . .
Wealthy women in 16th-century Europe thought it was fashionable to dye their teeth. In Italy, the most popular colors were red and green, while in Russia the favorite was black.

Stick your neck out!
Every bone in the body eventually stops growing. The last to do so is the collarbone.

Scientists say that the best time to take a nap is between 1:00 p.m. and 2:30 p.m. That's when a dip in body temperature makes you feel a little sleepy. So if you fall asleep in class, blame science.

Human hair is made up of a variety of elements.
There are even traces of gold in your hair.
Brunettes included!

Ouch! There are pain receptors all over the body.
**One square centimeter contains about
200 pain receptors.**

Everybody into the gene pool!
DNA is microscopic and takes up a small percentage
of the room in a cell. **If you put all the DNA in
the human body together, it would fit inside
a space about the size of an ice cube.**

What an air hog!
The brain is the single biggest consumer of oxygen.
It uses a quarter of all the oxygen in the body.

Burn your tongue? *No need for a bandage.*
**The tongue is the fastest-healing part
of the human body**.

The choice is yours:
Smiling requires the use of 17 muscles.
Frowning needs 43 muscles.

Your own private ocean inside . . .
Not only is **blood** mostly water, but the plasma
is almost as salty as ocean water.

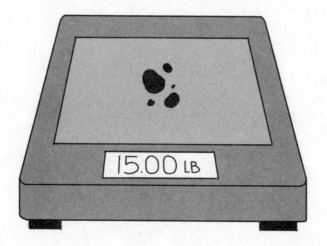

The weight of your blood makes up about
7 percent of your total body weight.
That's heavy stuff!

Baaaad blood?

The first successful blood transfusion took place in 1667.
A French doctor named Jean-Baptiste Denys injected
sheep's blood into a 15-year-old boy.

Drink up!

**Your blood is 83 percent water,
your brain is about 75 percent water,** and
your bones are about a quarter water.

Time to bone up . . .

**The strongest bone in the human body is
the thigh bone.** It's actually stronger than concrete.

Even the little ones are an important part of the
team: 50 percent of your hand strength comes
from your pinkie finger.

Your brain gives off little bits of electricity, even while you're sleeping. During the night, it produces enough charge to power a light bulb. How enlightening!

Lights out!
Until the 20th century, humans slept about 10 hours a night. Today we only sleep an average of seven. What happened? The development of electricity allowed us all to stay up later.

If you have metal tooth fillings and chew aluminum foil, it can generate a two-volt electrical current. *But please don't try this at home.*

Twins aren't always born in quick succession, or even on the same day. **The longest time between two twins being born was 87 days.** *Oh, baby!*

About one in every 2,000 newborn babies is born with at least one tooth already above the gums. *Now that's a baby tooth!*

Happy birthday, and happy Tuesday. **More babies are born on Tuesdays** than on any other day of the week.

The nose knows the difference. Just as everyone has a unique fingerprint, **we all have a unique (if barely detectable) scent.** Even identical twins have different scents.

People are taller when they wake up than when they go to bed. Gravity pulls you down a little bit over the course of the day. *Good morning, and my, have you grown!*

Stand tall! Stretch your arms out from side to side. **The distance from fingertip to fingertip is the same as your height.**

Everybody farts, every day. In fact, most people let out enough gas each day to fill up a small balloon. *Probably doesn't qualify for your science fair project, though!*

My, you have good taste in makeup!
Every time a person applies lipstick, they wind up swallowing a little bit. **Over the course of a lifetime, the average woman will consume four pounds of lipstick.**

A tapeworm is a parasite that can live and thrive inside the human intestines. It can grow to be about 30 feet long when all stretched out. That's roughly the length of a school bus!

Sensitive information: **There's a medical condition called *synesthesia*.** It mixes up senses, meaning people can see sounds, feel colors, or taste music.

Incoming . . .
Messages are sent from the nerves on your body to the brain—where they're processed—at a speed of about 200 miles an hour!

According to brain scans, when dogs and humans sleep together, they often dream at the same time. Man's best friend, even in Dreamland.

Ever wonder exactly how many calories you need to eat every day? The rule of thumb is that it's the number of your weight in pounds multiplied by 11.
Math can be delicious!

Feel the burn!
Your brain requires very little energy to operate. **It uses about 1/10 of a calorie per minute to function.**

According to studies of astronauts who have spent a lot of time in space, **fingernails and toenails grow more slowly in space than they do on Earth**.
So does a manicure cost less on Mars?

Transplants of most body parts are now possible.
You can even get a fingernail transplant.
Just don't bite 'em—the transplant often comes from a toenail.

Not everything is meant to be shared . . .
According to a survey, **10 percent of Americans
say they've picked someone else's nose.**

Scientists would call "brain freeze" or an
"ice cream headache" by its scientific name
of sphenopalatine ganglioneuralgia.
That name alone could make your head hurt.

You 'll walk an equivalent of three trips around the world in your lifetime. Just not all at once, and you won't have to walk across oceans.

Pick me!
The finger used the most for nose picking
(at 65 percent) is the index finger.
The least popular choice: the thumb (16 percent).

There's no single illness called "the cold."
Each year, many strains makes lots of people sick—about 100 different viruses are usually going around at one time.
That's something to sneeze at.

What a flake! Over your life,
you'll shed about 40 pounds of skin.
It comes off one flake at a time.

There's enough iron in your body to make a nail.
There's enough aluminum to make a piece of foil large
enough to wrap a cheeseburger.
Are you a robot?

Your tongue needs moisture to work. **If your tongue
is completely dry, your taste buds won't function.**
Water! Water!

Snot my fault!
Rhinotillexomania is the word for someone
who can't stop picking their nose.

Get out of the way! Sneezes travel at incredibly high speeds. They've been clocked as high as 994 miles per hour.

Skip the finger workout . . .
There aren't any muscles in your fingers, except the tiny *arrector pili* muscles that help make the hair on your fingers stand out straight. All finger movement is controlled by muscles in your arms.

You've got a lot of nerve . . . literally.
If you're average, there's a total of about **46 miles of nerves in your body.**

The Incredible Shrinking Brain is a true story.
Over the course of your lifetime, your brain does slowly shrink. It will decrease from its peak mass by about 15 percent.

Mosquitoes are more attracted to you if you've recently eaten a banana.
Yellow-no!

The longest recorded sneezing fit was 978 consecutive days.
Gesundheit! Gesundheit! Gesundheit . . .

The average human isn't completely "themselves."
We're all hosts to anywhere from two to nine pounds
of bacteria. Say hi to your guests!

Now hear this!
The part of your ear that sticks out isn't really where you hear. The hearing functions go on in the middle ear and the inner ear, which are safely stored inside the head.

There's a name for that feeling when you think there's a bug on you but there isn't. It's called *delusory parasitosis*. And it seems like siblings and jokey friends can bring it on.

Small but mighty!
The three smallest bones in the human body are all located inside the middle ear. The *stapes, malleus,* and *incus* put together could fit on top of a penny.

What is the purpose of earlobes? Scientists still aren't really sure.
They're just hanging around.

Add it all up and the average adult doesn't laugh all that much. Laughter totals about six minutes a day. *Make it your mission to change that with wacky facts from this book! Keep reading . . . .*

You can study in your sleep—sort of.
You'll recall the information better if you review it once and get a good night's sleep than if you were to stay up all night studying.

2
YOU'RE HISTORY

Discover some interesting stuff about interesting
things that happened long, long ago.

The only American president
who was both a licensed barber and
a former professional wrestler: Abraham Lincoln.

President James Garfield was an ambidextrous genius.
He could write in Latin with one hand and in Greek with
the other . . . at the same time!
Write on, man!

Borrow a dollar?
**The most valuable piece of money ever issued
in the U.S. was a $100,000 bill.** It was only
printed from 1934 to 1935.

Today, the largest bill in circulation is the $100 bill.
In 1969, the U.S. government got rid of all banknotes
worth more than that.
So, did they just throw them away?

Got change for a flower? In the 1630s, tulip bulbs
could be used as currency in Holland. The value varied
greatly: at its peak, a single tulip could be traded
for an entire estate. But when its value crashed,
one tulip was the price of an onion.

George Washington didn't have wooden teeth.
He had four sets of dentures (fake teeth), and they
were made from elephant ivory, hippo bone, and
human teeth, held together with golden springs.
Wood sounds better, actually.

Washington was lucky!
Dentures have been made for centuries.
Up until the 1800s, they were **usually made
from real teeth**, often those of dead people.

**Ancient Romans brushed their teeth,
but they didn't have toothpaste.**
They used powdered mouse brains as toothpaste.
Don't forget to floss!

**The first commercial for Charmin brand
toilet paper was** filmed in New York.
The studio was in a town called Flushing.
Makes perfect sense.

Just like "Yankee Doodle."
**In the 1700s, "macaroni" was a slang term
that meant "fashionable man."** It's an Italian word,
and Italy was thought to have the most
stylish people.

Out of this world!
**Cleopatra's lifespan was closer to the time of the
first moon landing** (in 1969 A.D.) than to the time
the Great Pyramid of Egypt was built
(around 2560 B.C.).

While Cleopatra ruled in ancient Egypt, she often wore a fake beard in public. Well, she was de queen of denial!

The world's first commercial communication satellite was *Intelsat I*. It was launched in 1965, and it's still in orbit. *Space is the place!*

Only one time has a satellite been wrecked by a passing meteor. A space rock killed the European Space Agency's *Olympus* in 1993. *Olympus has fallen!*

Not enough hours in the day?
The speed of the Earth's rotation changes over time. **A day in dinosaur times was only 23 hours long.**

The Canadian province of Nova Scotia doesn't want to displace historical artifacts. It's illegal to scavenge with a metal detector there, with a fine of $10,000. *Do not disturb!*

Pharaoh-really?
Think all of the pyramids are in Egypt?
Wrong—**there are more pyramids in Sudan than in Egypt.**

What's in a name?
West Virginia split off from Virginia in 1863.
It was almost named Kanawha, after an indigenous tribe.

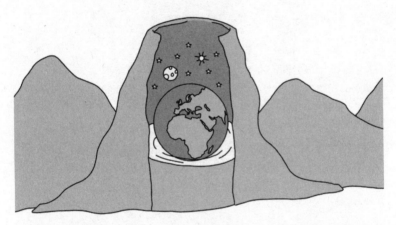

Ancient Babylonians thought that the Earth wasn't round but inside a hollow mountain, floating on a giant ocean. The sun, moon, sky, and stars were also inside the mountain. Hey, at least they didn't think it was flat.

Roll call!
Who was that Native American woman notable for her association with the colonial settlement at Jamestown, Virginia? **Pocahontas was just her nickname.** Her real name, given by her people, was Matoaka.

The original Bluebeard?
Archaeologists say the Great Sphinx of Egypt at one time had a red face and a blue beard. (It's faded over the years.)

A very attractive bit of trivia.
The ancient Greek philosopher Thales thought that magnets had souls. He figured that since they attracted and repelled each other, they were sort of alive.

Yeti is another name for Bigfoot.
In 1959, the U.S. government gave its embassy in the Asian country of Nepal a list of guidelines for how to safely hunt the Yeti there. They haven't found one yet-i.

When he died, Chinese emperor Qin Shi Huangdi (who ruled from 259 B.C to 210 B.C.) **wanted his body to be safe in case he ever came back to life**. So he had his tomb surrounded by 8,000 clay soldiers, 130 clay chariots, and 670 clay horses.
He still hasn't woken up.

When mummies were made in ancient Egypt, the brain had to be removed.
Mummy makers pulled it out through a nostril.
Next time you blow your nose, yell, "Brains!"

Archaeologists have found honey in the tombs of ancient Egyptian pharaohs. It was still edible.
So that means they tasted it?! Eww!

What's all the buzz?
In ancient Egypt, **slaves were ordered to smear themselves with honey** and stand near the pharaoh. Their job: to keep flies away from him.

President Ronald Reagan personally saved the lives of 77 people. When he was a young man, he worked as a lifeguard.
And they probably all voted for him.

Look at all the baby presidents!
What was it about the year 1946? During a 66-day period, future presidents Bill Clinton, George W. Bush, and Donald Trump were all born.

President Andrew Johnson was a self-taught tailor.
He made clothes both for himself and for his
closest political advisors.
The clothes make the man!

The White Zoo?
Past presidents had some pretty unusual pets.
Calvin Coolidge's animals included raccoons,
a pygmy hippo, and lion cubs. Herbert Hoover's son
owned a pair of alligators.
Teddy Roosevelt's family included a lizard, a pig, a bear,
and a one-legged rooster.

Not an Eagles fan.
Founding Father Benjamin Franklin didn't want the
eagle to be the national symbol of the United States.
He preferred the turkey.

In the 1860s, the state of Maryland had such a problem with boats from Virginia invading their shorelines to fish for oysters that the government formed an official "oyster navy" to defend the beaches. Was not sharing those oysters shellfish?

Time to moove out...
William Taft's cow, Pauline, was **the last cow to live at the White House**. She provided milk for him during his presidency.

The grand wooden desk in the Oval Office is made out of repurposed wood. It used to be part of an old U.S. Navy ship.
How a-boat that?

You're never too young . . . or old.
In 1975, 43-year-old **Donald Rumsfeld was appointed Secretary of Defense as the youngest person ever to hold the position**. In 2001, 68-year-old Rumsfeld was again appointed Secretary of Defense, and was the oldest person ever to hold the position.

Welcome to the jungle.
Navy SEALs are some of the most highly skilled and elite troops in the world. **When SEALs served in the Vietnam War, they wore pantyhose,** because it kept off the leeches that live in the jungle.

Strike a pose . . .
How statues of war heroes are posed reveals a lot about the person. If they're on a horse that has both front legs in the air, the person died in battle. If the horse has one front leg in the air, they died of wounds received in battle. If the horse has all four legs planted, the person died of natural causes.

King Alfonso IX ruled León (it's now part of France) from 1188 to 1230. When leading his troops, he'd get so riled up that he'd drool uncontrollably and foam at the mouth. That's why **he was known as Alfonso the Slobberer.**
You've got a little something on your face, your majesty.

How long did the **Hundred Years' War** between England and France last? ***Not* 100 years—it took place from 1337 to 1453.**
Then why not call it the 116 Years' War?

Go, Joe!
There was a "real American hero" named G.I. Joe.
He was a carrier pigeon during World War II.

Gotta have that morning pick-me-up.
The most popular way to drink coffee in Italy is as
a small cup of highly concentrated and caffeinated espresso.
**During World War II, Italian soldiers stationed in
North Africa carried their own individual espresso makers.**

Bacon bombs away!
**During World War II, the American Fat Salvage
Committee collected donated bacon fat from homes**.
It was used to make glycerin, which was used to make bombs.

The oldest alarm system:
Ancient Romans guarded their homes with guard dogs.
They even displayed "beware of dog" signs - whether
there were dogs on the property or not.

It's unknown who actually invented the fire hydrant. There was a patent . . . but it was destroyed in a fire.
If only they'd had a fire hydrant!

Everybody has to start somewhere.
Before he founded Microsoft, Bill Gates's first business was a company called Traf-O-Data. It automatically recorded the number of cars driving on streets.

The first cell phones were released in 1983.
The Motorola DynaTAC 8000x weighed four pounds and cost $4,000.
And you couldn't even use Instagram on it.

They're not just into teeth.
The electric chair was invented by a dentist.
So was cotton candy.

She just did it.
The Nike logo—the "Swoosh"—was designed by a college student named Carolyn Davidson. She was paid $35 at the time, but Nike later gave her more than $600,000 worth of free shoes.

Faster! Faster!
The first roller coaster in America opened at Coney Island in New York in 1884. Known as a switchback railway, it was invented by LaMarcus Thompson and inspired by contraptions used to move coal. The coaster traveled only six miles per hour.

In the present-day world of the Internet, **humans collectively generate more data in two days than was created in all of history** up until the year 2003. *That's a lot of Snaps!*

A powerful fact.
There's more computing power in a smartphone than there was in the computers that sent man to the moon. All of NASA's computers combined couldn't match what's in the average person's pocket.

When he visited France in the 1700s, **Thomas Jefferson snuck some rice seeds into his pockets and smuggled them back home.** That was highly illegal—if he'd been caught, he might have been put to death.
No, no, no, Mr. President!

Graffiti—art or messages drawn on a public building without permission—isn't a modern thing. **Archaeologists found graffiti on a wall dating to first-century Rome** that read "Successus was here."
Classic Successus!

Sure, Thomas Jefferson wrote the Declaration of Independence. But did you know that he also invented the swivel chair? Wheeeeeee!

Where there's a Will, there's a way.
During his lifetime, **Shakespeare's last name was spelled 83 different ways.**

Pull up your [BEEEEP!]
In 19th-century England, **"pants" was considered a very dirty word.**

Anyone have an eraser? Pennsylvania is spelled "Pensylvania" on the Liberty Bell. At the time, this spelling was one of several acceptable spellings for the state.

Not everybody wants to be president.
In 1952 Albert Einstein was offered the presidency of Israel. He turned down the offer.

Join the party!

For more than 150 years, every American president has been either a Republican or a Democrat.
The last president who wasn't was Millard Fillmore, a member of the Whig Party, who left office in 1853.

We're sure there's a scientific explanation for this. Albert Einstein made a lot of breakthroughs in science, but he always had cold feet. Einstein never wore socks.

Swinging from two branches!
William Howard Taft was president of the United States from 1909 to 1913. After he left office, he later got to hold his actual dream job: Chief Justice of the Supreme Court. **Taft is the only person to serve as both president and Chief Justice.**

Grover Cleveland is the only president to serve two terms not in a row, and **he's the only president who had an artificial jaw.** In 1893, he needed to have part of his jaw removed because of a tumor, and it was replaced with one made of rubber.
Bionic president!

Get a leg up.
"Shanks" are another name for legs. **King Edward I of England (he ruled from 1272 to 1307) had such long legs** that his nickname was Longshanks.

A speedy recovery.
In 1947, test pilot **Chuck Yeager got his plane up to 767 mph, breaking the sound barrier.**
Two days earlier, he broke two ribs when he fell off a horse.

Merrily, merrily, merrily . . . In 1968 and 1969, **a British man named Robin Knox-Johnson became the first person to sail around the world without stopping.**
It took him 313 days.

Yeah, that's pretty "Great."
The Great Pyramid in Egypt took 100,000 workers and 20 years to construct. It's made from an estimated 2.3 million limestone blocks.

It's not a stretch!
The Great Wall of China is over 13,000 miles long.
If it were stretched out in a straight line, it would reach from the North Pole to the South Pole.

The first known zoo was built in China in approximately 1900 B.C. It was called the Park of Intelligence.
What a smart idea!

Taking it to the streets!
Concrete has been around since ancient Roman times.
They made it out of lime, water, and volcanic ash.

Don't topple the tower!
The Eiffel Tower is one of the most famous buildings in the world, but it was almost demolished in 1909.
In the end, the French government decided it could be used as a radio tower and kept it around.

This one is golden.
Only about 165,000 tons of gold have been mined from the earth in recorded history. Put all together, it would form a cube of only 20 cubic meters.

Czar Nicholas II ruled over Russia from 1894 to 1917.
At one point, **Nicholas wanted to build an electric fence around the entire country.**
What a "powerful" idea.

In 1453, Greek forces in the city of Constantinople fell to the Turkish army. It was a Tuesday, and ever since, **Tuesdays are considered unlucky in Greece.**
Mondays aren't so great either.

Watch those apples...
In Ancient Greece, throwing an apple to a woman
was considered a marriage proposal. If the woman
caught the apple, she accepted.

Twice the presents?
Queen Elizabeth II of England has two birthdays.
She celebrates her real one privately on April 21.
Then she has an "official" one that's celebrated
with a parade in June, because April in England
is too cold for a parade.

Queen Berengaria ruled England in the 1890s.
Yet she never lived in or even visited England,
preferring to stay in what is today France.
Moving is such a bother.

In 18th-century Paris, street vendors sold baths.
They'd carry tubs and water into people's homes.
And then they'd make a clean break!

**King Alfonso of Spain was deaf, so he employed
a guy to nudge him when the national anthem
was playing.** That way, he knew when to salute.
Here's to you, King Alfonso, for thinking outside the box!

**The legendary composer Ludwig van Beethoven
lost his hearing when he was 45, but he kept
writing music.** He'd clench a stick in his teeth and
hold it against his piano's keyboard, enabling him
to make out faint sounds and vibrations.
Art finds a way.

He's got the skills that pay the bills.
Leonardo da Vinci was a painter, scientist,
mathematician, architect, and writer. But the talent
of which da Vinci was most proud: He could bend
iron with his bare hands.

Probably Leonardo da Vinci's most famous work was his painting the *Mona Lisa.* **In Italian, the *Mona Lisa*'s real name is *La Gioconda,*** which means "joyous woman."
Guess she wasn't the big smiley type.

He was on a first-name basis with the entire world.
Another famous Italian Renaissance artist was Michelangelo. **His full name was Michelangelo di Lodovico Buonarroti Simoni.**

Cable news network CNN (it stands for Cable News Network) was founded in 1980. **One of CNN's creators was named William Headline**.
Well, that's the name of the game.

The word *berserk* comes from Berserkers—Viking warriors who dressed in bearskins and howled during battle like they were wild animals.
Berserk indeed!

Kids . . . in . . . space!
The dwarf planet Pluto was discovered in 1930 by astronomer Clyde Tombaugh. **Naming it "Pluto" was the suggestion of 11-year-old Venetia Burney**.

Snow kidding! On February 18, 1979, it snowed in the Sahara Desert. But it only lasted for about half an hour.

Was it a triple-dog dare?
In 1859, daredevil Charles Blondin became the **first to walk across Niagara Falls on a tightrope**. The walk was technically 160 feet above the Niagara gorge, just down river from the Falls, so some say it didn't count until Nik Wallenda tightrope-walked directly over Niagara Falls, not downstream from it, in 2012.

The winter of 1848 was especially cold in the northeastern United States. **It was so cold that Niagara Falls briefly froze over, with no flowing water**.
Okay, that is *pretty cold.*

Moving day?
As the result of a February 2010 earthquake,
the city of Concepcion, Chile, shifted 10 feet west.

Delicious but deadly!
On January 15, 1919, **Boston was hit by a sticky tidal wave**
when a 50-foot-tall tank holding 2.3 million gallons of
molasses burst. The flood waters rose as high as 25 feet,
killing 21 people and injuring 150 more. Cleanup lasted
for weeks.

Alexander Graham Bell invented the telephone.
But he never telephoned his wife or mother
because they were both hearing-impaired.

Philip Griebel was a German potter. In the 1800s,
he invented the garden gnome. Gnome is where
the heart is.

You look familiar.
In medieval times, people didn't travel much out
of their hometown. **The average person met
about 100 other people in their entire life.**

Sorry, Columbus.
**The first European explorer to visit North America
was Leif Eriksson.** He was a Viking, and he came to
the New World in about 1000 A.D.

The U.S. bought Alaska from Russia in 1867.
It cost only two cents an acre.
What a deal!

Down Under and through the woods . . .
**Native Australians didn't have maps, but they mapped
out the entire continent.** They wrote and memorized
songs about landmarks, including rocks, trees, and rivers.

This fact rules!
**The only country left on earth that still calls
itself an empire is Japan.** Its current emperor,
the 125th in its history, is named Akihito.

The British Empire was the largest empire of all time.
By 1922, it covered a fifth of the world's land.
Which is a lot of land.

**The first country to give women the right to vote:
New Zealand, in 1893.** Switzerland didn't let women
vote until 1971.
Sheesh, Switzerland!

Get out the vote!
The U.S. didn't officially give women
voting rights until 1920, but some women in colonial
times voted. **The first woman to vote in North America
was Lydia Chapin Taft.** In 1756, she cast a ballot
in a Massachusetts Colony election.

The first female elected prime minister: Sirimavo
Bandaranaike of Sri Lanka. She first served from
1960 to 1965.
The first of many!

3
GOING WILD

Get back to nature with these amazing facts about the animal kingdom, the world of plants, and bugs.

What's so funny? The "laugh" of a laughing hyena can be heard from as far as three miles away.

Australia is a great place to camp. Why?
No bears are native to the continent.
What about koalas, though? Koalas aren't
technically bears—they're marsupials, like kangaroos.
(That means they have pouches.)

African elephants carry their young for 640 days,
or about 22 months before giving birth,
the longest gestation of any mammal.
That's a long wait for a birthday!

Got a pet squid? *Cool!* Make sure to keep it cold.
Squids can suffocate in warm water.

Gesundheit! Certain species of iguanas get rid of
excess levels of salt in their bodies by sneezing it out.

It's a myth that all piranhas are ravenous flesh-eaters. Actually, only a few of the many species of piranha are. The vast majority eat plants and insects. But we don't recommend testing which species you're dealing with.

A lobster's blood is colorless. But when it's exposed to oxygen in the air, it turns blue.
What a blue blood!

What a big heart you have!
A blue whale's heart weighs 400 pounds.
Even though it's only about 1 percent of the whale's body weight, it's still the biggest on the planet.

Speak!
The Basenji is a breed of dog that whines,
chatters, and yodels. But it **can't bark.**

Most dogs can recognize around 165 words, and
smarter breeds up to 250. That's about as smart as
a two-year-old child.
Plus they're potty-trained.

The Catalburun is a breed of dog native to Turkey
that looks like a really big basset hound. It's also the only
dog in the world **with a split nose.** There's a line right down
the middle, with a nostril on each side.
Sounds like a nosy little pupper.

Dogs can smell fear—and anxiety. When we
have those feelings, we sweat very lightly and
dogs can smell that.
That's ruff.

Dogs have 300 million smell receptors.
Humans have only six million.
Now you nose.

A human's fingerprint is unique.
A dog's "snout print" is equally unique.
But they're all always wet!

The fleshy, squishy-faced Chow Chow is a dog that
originated in China. **The Chow Chow is the only dog
in the world that has a naturally purple tongue.**
It looks grape!

(Ceremonial) Mayor of Cormorant, Minnesota:
a dog named Duke. He's a Great Pyrenees
achieving greatness.

Rodents will eat pretty much anything, but they don't necessarily crave cheese. **Studies show they actually prefer peanut butter.**
You can catch them in a Jif-fy.

Spin that wheel!
A hamster runs at a speed equal to one 2000th horsepower.

You may not want to wait around, staring in its eyes, but . . .
Most venomous snakes have oval-shaped pupils.
Most nonvenomous snakes have round pupils.

HA HA HA!

Elmo isn't alone!
According to a University of Washington study,
rats laugh when tickled.

Size doesn't matter in this fight.
Rattlesnake venom is deadly, but so is black widow venom. **The spider stuff is 15 times more potent** than the snake stuff.

Bees love the nectar in citrus flowers.
Why? It contains caffeine, enough to get a bee, well, *buzzed.*

A bite from a lone star tick can leave the victim permanently allergic to red meat. Why can't it be brussels sprouts?

Honeybee Weather

Sunday	Monday	Tuesday	Wednesday	Thursday	Friday	Saturday
95°	95°	95°	95°	95°	95°	95°

The hive forecast shows honey with a high of 95. Honeybee hives are always about 95 degrees Fahrenheit. Now that's a hot place to work!

Shoo!
When flies land on food, they vomit enzymes and saliva. Those break the food down so they can lick it up with their tongues.

Lights out!
Why do moths fly into lights?
Scientists actually have no idea why.

Makes cents.
A hummingbird weighs about .05 ounces. That's less than a penny.

Hey, Mom and Dad!
Baby Eurasian Roller Birds sense danger
and vomit orange stuff to warn their parents.

Who?
If you look deep into an owl's ear, **you can actually see the back of its eyeball.**

Special delivery:
Bats can deliver their babies in midflight.
The mother gives birth and then quickly swoops down and catches the little one.

People who eat bugs say that beetles taste like apples. Worms apparently taste like bacon. *We'll take their word for it.*

Why should bees get all the fun?
Bats work the night shift to pollinate peaches, bananas, cashews, and avocados.

Don't ask us how we know,
but termites reportedly taste like carrots.

Carrots aren't the best food for rabbits.
They're pretty high in sugar and should be used
as once-in-a-while treats. People link carrots and
rabbits because of Bugs Bunny—who was imitating
a character from *It Happened One Night,* a popular
movie in the 1930s.
That's what's up, doc.

Get on my lawn!
There are about twice as many plastic flamingos
decorating yards in the U.S. than there are real ones flying
around.

Penguins mate for life. They'll even propose to one another by giving each other a pebble.
With this rock, I thee wed.

How can you tell a male turkey from a female turkey?
If the turkey gobbles, it's a boy.
Happy Thanksgiving!

Your local zoo may accept your old Christmas tree.
Why? Some animals like to eat them.
It's like a giant candy cane for them.

When frogs hibernate, their bodies "freeze" over.
They stop breathing and only stay alive due to huge reservoirs of food in their bloodstream, which prevents their organs from shutting down.
Otherwise, they'd . . . croak.

The better to see you with.
Crocodiles sleep with their eyes open.

That hard-to-notice, sneaky wave called a rip current is one of the deadliest things in the ocean. **It's 45 times more likely to attack you than a shark is.**
Don't let 'er rip.

Its heart is in the right place, believe it or not.
Where would you find **the heart of a shrimp?**
Inside its head.

Time to bone up on your cat knowledge.
A cat's tail has a surprisingly large number
of bones in it. In fact, **10 percent of all
the bones in a cat's body are in the tail.**

Little brain, big bite:
A great white shark's brain weighs about 34 grams,
roughly the weight of a couple of graham crackers.

Humans can't drink salt water, but cats can.
They have incredibly efficient kidneys that filter
out all the salt from the water.
Ah, we sea!

Do you have sweaty paws?
Cats don't have human-style sweat glands.
If they need to cool off, they sweat through their paws.

Cheetahs aren't just the fastest land animal on earth—
they're also incredibly agile. When jumping through the air,
they can change direction in the middle of the leap.
Hey, that's cheetah-ing!

A lion's roar is much louder than you probably think
it is. If you ran 25 lawnmowers at the same time,
that would equal the sound level of one lion's roar.

**The bearcat, which lives in tropical Southeast Asia,
smells like buttered popcorn.** The scent comes from
a gland located just underneath its tail.
That's wild!

Now hear this:
A giraffe's tongue is 21 inches long.
The giraffe can use it to clean out its own ears.

Hey, don't sweat it.
Human sweat is basically clear, but that's
not the case for all animals. For example,
the sweat of a hippopotamus is red.

Go on, it will wait.
A scorpion can hold its breath for up to six days.

A Russell's viper bite makes blood instantly clot. It turns
it from liquid into something with the consistency of jelly.
And it tastes terrible on toast.

More than just a name . . .
A jumping spider really can jump—up to
40 times its body length.

Texas horned lizards have a unique defense against
predators: They squirt blood from their eyes.
Talk about giving the evil eye!

If a cockroach touches a human, it will run away.
And then it thoroughly cleans itself.
Wait, so they think we're gross?!

A fintastic fact:
Marine biologists noticed that when dolphins were near each other, they used a specific whistle to identity one another. In other words, **dolphins kind of have names.**

Birds don't have bladders to store urine.
When it's processed, they just release it immediately.
When they gotta go, look out below!

Meet you in my dreams?
Sea otters are one of the most adorable animals out there, and the way they sleep makes them even cuter. **Otters hold hands while they sleep** so they don't get separated from one another.

Have a special greeting with your tribe?
It probably doesn't top the white capuchin monkeys'.
They stick their fingers up each other's noses.

How big is a fully grown koala?
About the same size as a newborn polar bear.
Bear's the difference.

What a find!
**The largest pearl ever discovered
weighed 75 pounds.** A fisherman in the Philippines
found it in a giant clam in 2006 . . . and kept it
hidden under his bed for 10 years!

Coral looks like rocks, but it's a living thing. It reproduces
very rarely, only in the week after a full moon.
OK, coral.

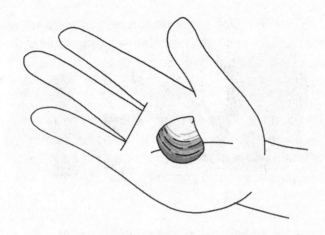

Still got some growing to do...
A deep sea clam reaches the size of
1/3 inch long after about 100 years.

Not just chameleons: Octopuses and seahorses can
also change color to blend in with their environments.
Ever been in a situation where wish you could
do the same?

From 1987 to 1994, **Japanese researchers studied whether earthquakes are caused by catfish wiggling their tails.** As it turns out, earthquakes are *not* caused by that. *Good to know!*

Walruses don't seem to do much when they're awake, but they do need to sleep. **When it's time for bed, they inflate a *pharyngeal pouch*** inside their body, which keeps them floating on the ocean while they sleep. *Now that's a waterbed!*

Fish don't have eyelids—all except for the fugu. It's the only fish that can close its eyes. So *what would a fish dream about?*

Hey, melonhead!
A bottlenose dolphin's forehead is called a "melon."

While elephants are the largest land mammals and many times larger than people, **their eyes are only about the same size as people's.**
Well, that's a surpr-eyes!

Good kitty?
There are an estimated 6,000 tigers in the United States . . . being kept as pets in people's homes.

But they don't taste like oranges.
Bison usually have brown fur and skin, but they aren't born that way. **When they're babies, they're orange.**

Koalas reportedly smell like cough drops. The reason: They eat eucalyptus leaves, which is a main ingredient in cough drops.
Or at least in the high-koala-ty ones.

From "Ouch!" to "That smells great!"
When it stings, a honeybee releases a chemical into the air that smells like bananas. It's an alarm signal sent out to other bees.

Say what?
Not all bees buzz. **Some honeybee queens have been observed quacking** like ducks.

There's a reason why "slothful" means "lazy."
A sloth isn't just slow at moving around. It will also take up to two weeks to digest a meal.

What's for dinner ~~tonight~~ this month?
Komodo dragons only need to eat about
12 times a year.

In her lifetime, **a dairy cow will produce about
200,000 glasses of milk.** That requires her to drink
30 gallons of water every day.
That's enough to fill a bathtub!

It's the law!
Pigs are very intelligent animals and
can get bored. **In England, farmers have
to provide toys for their pigs to play with.**

It's illegal to hunt swans in England. **That's because
they all officially belong to the Queen.**
Just one of the benefits of being queen.

**The honorary Colonel-in-Chief of the Norwegian
King's Guard** is named Sir Nils Olav. **And he is a penguin.**
He looks great in the black-and-white uniform.

Words for bird nerds:
**When a group of geese is on the ground,
it's called a *gaggle*.**
But if the group is flying in the air, it's called a *skein*.

Coming through!
Why do geese honk when they're flying? It's to let
other geese know they're there, and to get out of the way.

Not quite King Kong...
The largest primate in history was a prehistoric ape
that lived in present-day China called the
gigantopithecus. It stood over 10 feet
tall and weighed 1,200 pounds.

They really had a bird's eye view.
On the first hot air balloon flight in 1783, there were only
three passengers. They were **a duck, a rooster, and a sheep.**

A 78-foot-tall cactus in Arizona was the tallest in history. Or it was until 1986, when the 150-year-old plant was knocked over in a windstorm.
Weather you like it or not.

The most dangerous (and poisonous) plant in North America is the water hemlock.
Even touching it can be deadly.
So don't touch it!

Ring around . . . the tree stump?
You can tell how old many types of tree are by counting the rings in their stumps.
The rings form when a tree goes dormant and stops growing in the winter. Trees in the rainforest don't stop growing, so they don't have rings.

There are billions and billions of stars in the Milky Way galaxy.
There are more trees than that on earth.
They're the real stars here.

Who needs a lawn mower anyway?
On Google's campus in northern California,
all the grass cutting is performed by a flock of 200 goats. They chew the grass down to the proper length.

Do they really need all of those?
Slugs have 3,000 teeth. They also have four noses.

If a newt loses a limb, it can regrow it.
It takes about 10 weeks.
That's 10 weeks well spent.

Heads (and noses) up!
A skunk can spray its smelly stench as far as 10 feet. And it can spray it accurately onto a target.

The eastern spotted skunk does a little something that lets humans and other animals know it's about to spray: **a handstand.**
Don't say we didn't warn you!

Wombat poop is cube-shaped.
That way it doesn't roll,
which makes it great for marking territory.

Africa is home to the striped polecat, or zorilla.
It sprays predators, and the smell has been compared
to vomit.
Smell ya later!

The roadkill reality show:
When an opossum plays dead, it *really* plays dead.
Not only does it lie perfectly still, but it also lets out
an odor that smells just like rotting meat!

Eulachon are a very oily type of fish.
**Some Native American groups would catch them,
insert wicks, and use them as candles.**
Would you want a fish-scented candle?

How do parrot fish fend off parasites?
They sleep in a mucus cocoon.
Goodnight!

All bets are off.
An alligator's brain is tiny.
It's about the size of a poker chip.

Penguins can be tickled. And they'll laugh.
Koochie-koochie-koo!

South African giant bullfrogs are big for frogs—about
the size of a puppy—but they're not *that* big. They've
been known to attack lions.
Which can't be a very good idea.

Some 400 million years ago, mushrooms were as tall as trees. Imagine the powerups in Mario Kart!

"Big" dinosaur fan?
The *Amphicoelias fragillimus* is believed to be the biggest dinosaur that ever existed.
It was 190 feet long and weighed a quarter of a million pounds.

Dream on!
Snails have been known to sleep for as long as **three years at a time.**

Ever wonder how baby chicks stay alive while trapped inside a shell, just before they hatch? **There are tiny holes in an eggshell—the developed chick can breathe through it.** *Now that's something to cluck about.*

Rats off!
Rats are native to Asia. They've spread to every corner of the world through ships.

Tailspin!
A beaver's huge, flat tail slapping on the water makes a lot of noise. The sound can be heard from as far as half a mile away.

Meet the beetles!
The one creature that there's more of than any other on earth: beetles.

This one sounds like a stretch, but it's totally true.
A slug can stretch itself out to about 20 times its regular body length.

4
VERY ENTERTAINING

We hope these facts about the world of entertainment—movies, TV, music, gaming—are, well, entertaining!

What a deal! There are trillions of possibilities for how a shuffled deck of cards will turn out. There are so many that it's likely each time they're shuffled that they'll be in a combination that has never occurred before.

In chess, the game is over when one player captures the other player's king. They say "checkmate," which comes from the Persian phrase *shah mat*, meaning "the king is frozen."
Wait, it doesn't mean "Ha ha, I won"?

That's a yes . . . and yes again!
A Ouija board doesn't really communicate with ghosts.
It's a board game that allows players to pretend to ask ghosts
yes-or-no questions. The name Ouija is a combination of
"yes" in French (*oui*) and . . . "yes" in German (*ja*).

***Harry Potter* author J.K. Rowling's actual first name**
is Joanne. She doesn't have an official middle name,
according to her birth certificate. But her publishers
wanted two initials, so she used "K" for Kathleen,
which was the first name of her grandmother.
No expecto middle name!

The magician Harry Houdini was a master escape artist.
As a kid, Houdini frequently broke into his family's
locked cookie cabinet. Talk about getting
an early start.

Do you have swagger?
Well, then you can thank William Shakespeare.
The famous playwright invented the word
way back in the 1600s.

Read it and weep . . . like Moaning Myrtle!
Harry Potter was rejected by 12 different publishers.
They all thought it was too difficult for children.

Books are probably more popular in Iceland
than anywhere else. Per capita, the tiny country
leads the world in books written, sold, and read.
One in 10 Icelanders will even publish a book.
Do they have no shelf control?

Good choice:
In 1969, author Eric Carle was punching holes in some paper when he imagined a bookworm eating through a book. His publisher suggested a caterpillar instead. **The Very Hungry Caterpillar has since sold over 30 million copies.**

It has to be Wendy to fly?
J.M. Barrie made up the name Wendy for his play, and then book, *Peter Pan*. People have been naming their daughters that ever since.

Good ol' Charlie Brown just *barely* tolerates Peppermint Patty.
(She's the one who calls him Chuck.)
Creator Charles Schulz got the idea for her name after looking at a dish of candy on his desk. Her full name is Patricia "Peppermint Patty" Reichardt.
How sweet!

In Denmark, *Peanuts* is known as *Radiserne,* which means "Radishes."
Well, a radish is kind of like a peanut . . .

Kiddie TV!
Youngest TV show host: Luis Tanner, host of the Australian show *Cooking for Kids with Luis*. He began hosting the show in 2004, when he was just six years old.

The first author in history to earn $1 million with his writing: Jack London, author of *The Call of the Wild*. Better start polishing up those English essays!

Wolfgang Amadeus Mozart began composing music as a child. At the age of 5!
Most of us were just writing our name . . . not so well!

We won't mention the auditions. . . .
***American Idol* has created lots of stars**,
like Kelly Clarkson and Katharine McPhee.
The most successful: Carrie Underwood, who has sold 14 million albums.

America's got (familiar) sound effects:
The sound effect used on *America's Got Talent*
when judges "check" an act was originally the sound
used when spins are passed on the game show
Press Your Luck. The sound effect used when judges
"X" an act is the strike sound used on *Family Feud.*

It looks a lot bigger on TV.
The "wheel" on *Wheel of Fortune* isn't that big.
It's only about seven feet long, edge to edge.

Pop singer Shakira was rejected from her grade
school choir. Her teacher thought she sounded
like a goat. You have goat to be kidding me!

Hulu.com, the streaming TV website, got its name from a Mandarin Chinese word with two meanings: "hollowed-out gourd" and "interactive recording." *Wonder which one it refers to. . . .*

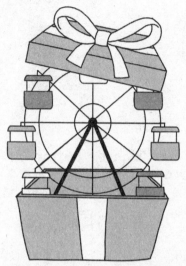

Come on down! The TV game show
The Price is Right gives away a lot of odd prizes.
One time, it awarded a contestant a Ferris wheel.

Are you still ~~watching~~ reading?
It's hard to imagine Netflix not being Netflix. **But before it took on that name,** the movie company thought about calling itself Kibble, Luna, Replay, or Directpix.

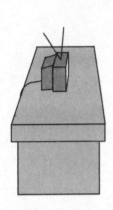

The world's first high-definition TV screen, built in 1984, was only two inches wide. But at least the picture was clear.

Join the bandwidth!
From 7 to 9 p.m., a third of all internet traffic in the U.S. is from Netflix.

Actor Will Ferrell turned down the chance to star in a sequel to *Elf*. He also passed on a $29 million paycheck to do so.
Big money for a "small" movie.

It would have been a thriller!
The late pop star Michael Jackson wanted to produce a *Harry Potter* musical. J.K. Rowling wouldn't let him.

Food theaters?

Movie theaters don't get most of their money from the movies.

The money from tickets goes to the movie studios, while the theater gets its money from selling popcorn and candy.

The story that's been made into a movie the most times: *Dracula*. That's not even counting all the other vampire movies. Filmmakers just really like to "sink their teeth" into it!

The most expensive movie ever made was 2011's *Pirates of the Caribbean: On Stranger Tides*. It cost more than $400 million to produce. *They reached Depp into their pockets.*

John Williams has composed the musical score for every big *Star Wars* movie. He has also never seen any of the finished *Star Wars* movies.
He has stayed in a galaxy far, far away.

Ewan McGregor starred as Obi-Wan Kenobi in some *Star Wars* movies. When he filmed his lightsaber battles, the director needed to tell him he didn't need to make the "whoosh" sound while he acted.
May the force be (silent) with you!

Movie theater popcorn is extremely expensive.
Ounce for ounce, it costs more to buy a tub than
it does to buy a filet mignon in a fancy restaurant.
Anyone thinking snacks after the show?

George Lucas created *Star Wars*. **When he came up with the idea, he called it** *Adventures of Luke Starkiller, as Taken from the Journal of the Whills, Saga I: The Star Wars. Rolls right off the tongue, doesn't it?*

In the original *Star Wars* trilogy, four guys played Darth Vader. Actor David Prowse was in the suit, James Earl Jones provided the voice, Sebastian Shaw played his revealed face, and a fourth, unknown person did the ominous breathing.
That's a lot of Darths!

In the *Star Wars* movies, Yoda was designed to look like famous scientist Albert Einstein.
Inspiration he was!

Brother actors Chris Hemsworth and Liam Hemsworth auditioned to play Thor in the Marvel Comics movies. Their other brother, Luke, has a cameo in *Thor: Ragnarok* as an actor playing Thor.
It's the family business.

In 2016, actor Tom Holland won the role of Spider-Man. He found out when the rest of the world did: when Marvel posted the news on Instagram.
His Spidey-sense wasn't tingling.

What a kick! Actor Leonardo DiCaprio was named after the famous artist Leonardo da Vinci. His mother was in Italy looking at a da Vinci painting when she felt her baby kick for the first time.

He is Groot.
For *Guardians of the Galaxy Vol. 2*, Vin Diesel, who voices Groot, was actually given a script explaining what every "I am Groot" meant. Only he and director James Gunn ever saw it.

"She should just pick two and let's go."
There were 289,240,840 key animation frames created for the film *Finding Dory*. A key animation frame defines pivotal points of motion in a sequence.

Keep an eye out . . .
Sid, the toy-torturing neighbor in the first *Toy Story* Movie, has a cameo role in *Toy Story 3* as a garbage collector.

Hey, Nick!
The first movie theaters were called nickelodeons—entry cost five cents. The first one opened in McKeesport, Pennsylvania, in 1905.

The hard truth: So much metal was being used to make tanks and bombs during World War II that there was a shortage.
So **the Oscars movie awards issued during those years were made of wood.**

Back when movies were starting to get popular in the 1920s, **the first movies with sound in them were called "talkies," while documentary films were called "actualities."**
And that is "actually" true!

When movie extras in the background are supposed to be talking, they say either "walla-walla" or "watermelon" quietly to themselves.
To do it out loud would be ridiculous!

The first 3-D movie was called *House of Wax*, and it hit theaters in 1953. The director only had one eye, so he couldn't make out the 3-D effects.
(Don't watch it—*it's a pretty scary movie.*)

Wow! Wow!
Before she wrote *The Hunger Games*, Suzanne Collins wrote for the TV show *Wow! Wow! Wubbzy!*

He was a real spy-hard.
The character of James Bond is based on William Stephenson, a real-life Canadian spy.

Oh? No!
The first James Bond movie, *Dr. No*, was released in Japan under a title that translates to "We Don't Want a Doctor."

In the science-fiction series *Doctor Who,* the lead character is called The Doctor. **His real name is actually Christoreslvdespovratorcovor De Lungborrow.** *Now that's a mouthful.*

Can you even imagine her having another name?
Well, **Barbie's full name** is Barbara Millicent Roberts.

Ever wonder what Muppets are made out of (besides magic)?
The frames are constructed out of a bendable, rubbery plastic called polyfoam. The fur is made out of fleece—puppet builders like it because it doesn't get fuzzballs and can be dyed almost any color.
It's easy being green.

What a wacky move . . .

Back in the '70s, Jim Henson liked Muppets' long, oval eyes to be made from Wacky Stacks, a toy line of plastic eggs. When Wacky Stacks went out of business, Henson bought the company's entire unsold inventory so he and his co-Muppeteeers would always have eye material.

The very first Barbie came with the very first Barbie outfit, of course. But surprisingly, it wasn't a bling-y gown. It was a black-and-white-striped swimsuit.

Like, wow, Scoob!

Scooby-Doo is just the cartoon dog's *nickname*. His real name is Scoobert.

Jim Henson's first Kermit the Frog was actually Kermit the...Lizard. He made it out of green material he got from cutting up an old coat his mother didn't want anymore. Double-check before cutting!

Winnie was just an affectionate nickname.
Winnie the Pooh's given name was Edward Bear.
"Edward Bear Sticks" just doesn't have the same ring to it.

We think we'll stick with Snuffy.
On *Sesame Street*, Big Bird's best friend is Snuffy,
or Snuffleupagus. His real first name is Aloysius.

Does Mickey know?
Minnie can be a nickname for a lot of names.
For Minnie Mouse, it's short for Minerva.

A fine-feathered friend:
Donald Duck has a middle name. It's Fauntleroy.

Mickey who?
Walt Disney's first cartoon character
wasn't Mickey Mouse. It was Oswald the Lucky Rabbit.

In Italy, Mickey Mouse is known as Topolino.
That literally translates to "Baby Mouse."
Who knew he was so young?

Forgery!
Walt Disney's actual signature didn't look
anything like the Disney logo. That one was created by
an artist.

In 1991, Wayne Allwine, the longtime voice of
Mickey Mouse, married Russi Taylor, the longtime
voice of Minnie Mouse. Imagine the conversations.

It was his secret weapon.
After the *Popeye* comic strip launched in 1931, spinach consumption went up by 33 percent.

***The Smurfs* started as a comic book.** When it was made into a TV cartoon and then a series of movies, some characters didn't make it, such as Alchemist Smurf, Finance Smurf, and Pastry Cook Smurf.
Didn't their la-la's measure up?

Here's a SMASH-ing revelation:
The Incredible Hulk was originally gray, not green.

Look, up in the sky, it's . . . a guy in a brown suit!
To get the tones for the costume on the black-and-white TV series *Adventures of Superman* just right, producers used brown and gray fabrics.

When Jerry Siegel and Joe Shuster first came up with Superman in 1932, he was a bad guy. In the first-ever *Superman* story, a mad scientist transforms a regular guy named Bill Dunn into Superman, who can control other people's minds. Superman kills the mad scientist, uses his psychic powers to make millions off the stock market, and then loses it all.
Not so super.

How did Yahtzee get its name? A Canadian couple invented it on their yacht.
And then they presumably yelled "Yahtzee!"

At least the equipment is free.
You can play Rock, Paper, Scissors professionally.
There's an official league in the United States.

More Monopoly money is printed each year
than actual, legal money: about $50 billion.
That's a lot of greenbacks (and pinkbacks and
whitebacks and yellowbacks . . .).

The highest-grossing video game of all time:
World of Warcraft. Since being released in 2004,
it's earned its creators more than $10 billion.
"Yeah, Mom, I'm studying . . . how to be a millionaire."

"It's-a-me, Jumpman"?
When the video game character of Mario made
his first appearance in the video game *Donkey Kong*,
he wasn't named Mario yet. In the game's manual, he was
just named Jumpman, because he jumped a lot.

The landlord of Nintendo's first warehouse in the United States was named Mario Segale. The company named Jumpman after him. And a character was born. *Did that come with a discount on rent?*

Princess of video games:
The Mario universe character Princess Peach is the most common female character in video game history. She's appeared in more than 60 games since 1985.

The Nintendo PlayStation?
The PlayStation was first developed as a new Nintendo gaming system, but with parts made by Sony. Nintendo decided to scrap the idea, so Sony made the console itself, which went on to become the bestselling video game system of all time.

Well, yellow there!
Creators of *The Simpsons* colored characters' skin yellow so they'd catch the eye of people flipping through the channels.
(It worked.)

Now here's some incredibly useful information:
Homer Simpson's PIN—for his bank card—is 7431.

When *Bob's Burgers* creator Loren Bouchard thought up the show, he intended it to be a lot different. He wanted it to be about a family of cannibals. *Check please!*

There's always a catch . . . .
SpongeBob was originally called SpongeBoy,
but that name was already taken (copyrighted, in fact)
by a mop product. In one episode, you can catch
Mr. Krabs call SpongeBob "SpongeBoy, me bob!"

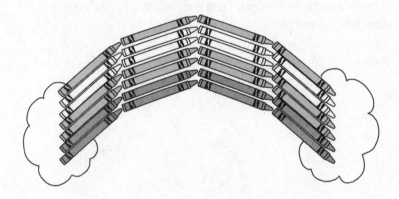

Every color in the rainbow...and then some!
There used to be only eight Crayola crayon colors;
now there are more than a hundred. Every 28 years,
the number of colors available doubles.

Put 32 candles on that cake!
As of this year, **SpongeBob SquarePants is
32 years young.** According to his driver's license
shown on the show, he was born on July 14, 1986.

Switcheroo!
**Nolan Gould, who plays the not-so-smart
Luke on *Modern Family*,** is a genius in real life.

How rude!
Actress Soni Nicole Bringas who plays Romana Gibbler on *Fuller House* didn't grow up watching the original show. But once she got the part, she watched all of the series in a month.

Tyler Joseph of Twenty One Pilots says his favorite concert moment was actually a time when absolutely no one in the audience was watching them play. Their focus: a guy dressed in a gingerbread-man costume, crowd surfing. *Tyler says he didn't blame them.*

Taylor Swift grew up on a Christmas tree farm. Her job was to knock praying mantises off the trees. Shake 'em off, shake 'em off.

What is he, a rocket scientist?
Close. **Both the mother and father of actor/musician Jack Black** were rocket scientists.

There's a heavy metal band called Hatebeak, unique in that its lead singer is a parrot. He can really rock back and forth!

Zendaya can't *just* act, sing, and hip-hop dance. She also knows how to hula. She spent three years dancing in a dance group called Future Shock Oakland that did hip-hop and hula dances.
Add boxing to the list, and you could call her Hawaiian Punch!

The Grammy Awards hand out trophies each year to the best pop groups and rock bands. They were started in the 1950s to recognize "quality" orchestral and gentle music that record companies thought was being threatened by rock 'n' roll.
Whoops!

The Billboard Hot 100 #1 hits for the longest consecutive weeks: "One Sweet Day" from Mariah Carey and Boyz II Men topped the charts for 16 weeks in the mid-'90s, and Luis Fonsi's "Despacito" tied the record in 2017.
And we're still not sick of it!

In 1976, a musician named Rodrigo had a hit with "Guitar Concierto de Aranjuez." Due to a calculating error, **it was only #1 in England for three hours.**
Now that's a short tune.

She had a million reasons why. Lady Gaga taught herself how to play the piano. She did that when she was only four years old.

When Beethoven would sit down to compose, he'd get his creative energies going by dumping ice water on his head. *Well, that's one way to do it.*

The first electric guitar was shaped kind of funny, like a frying pan - so much so that it was named the Frying Pan. And, boy, could it "cook."

What an interesting "writr."
In 1969, French writer Georges Perec wrote *La Disparition* (The Void) and three years later he wrote *Les Revenentes* (The Ghosts). The first book doesn't use the vowel "e" at all; in the second, "e" is the only vowel used.

***The Wizard of Oz* books were written by L. Frank Baum.**
He got the name "Oz" when he looked at his filing cabinet and saw the label "O–Z."
It sounds a lot better than "An."

When the film version of **The Wizard of Oz was released in 1939, it wasn't a hit and movie critics didn't like it.** They thought it was boring and uncreative. *Lions and tigers and munchkins and wizards . . . oh sigh!*

Totally spaced out! Halley's Comet passes by the Earth every 75 years or so. **Mark Twain, who wrote classic novels like The Adventures of Tom Sawyer,** was born on a day when the comet was visible in the sky, and he died when it was visible again 75 years later.

Wooden you like to know?
A violin is constructed from many small pieces of wood. The average one is made from 70 separate pieces.

The life of a dog!
Millie, a dog owned by President George H. W. Bush, made more money in 1991 than he did. She published a bestseller called *Millie's Book* that was actually written by First Lady Barbara Bush.

It was just his type.
**Mark Twain's *Tom Sawyer*
was the first novel** ever written on a typewriter.

He was a word nerd. . . .
Dr. Seuss coined the word "nerd."
He invented it for his 1950 book *If I Ran the Zoo*.

5
THE BALL'S IN YOUR COURT

Get your game on with these sporting facts about sports!

Push aside the couches!
The first - ever roller skating rink opened
in New York City in 1866...in a furniture store.

Bull's-eye!
The second-most popular sport on TV in England, after soccer: darts.

Let's go for a spin sometime.
Frisbees and other flying discs outsell baseballs, basketballs, and footballs combined.

According to Frisbee, if you throw one of its flying discs perfectly, it will spin exactly six times a second. But who's counting?!

Kite flying is a professional sport in Thailand.
So, let's go fly a kite!

Michael Jordan was cut from his high school basketball team.
But he went on to have a pretty good career.

Basketball legend Michael Jordan holds many records. But the most nutritious? Appearing on the most Wheaties boxes: a whopping 18 times.

Opposites attract:
During the 1987–88 season, Manute Bol and Muggsy Bogues were teammates on the Washington Bullets. **At the time, they were the tallest (7'7") and shortest (5'3") players in NBA history.**

Well, hop to it.
Until 1936, a jump ball was held after every successful basket in basketball. It took place at center court.

There are 10 "honorary" Harlem Globetrotters, including Pope John Paul II, Pope Francis, and Robin Roberts of *Good Morning America*. Unfortunately, none of them have ever gotten to take the court for the traveling team.

Stephen Curry of the Golden State Warriors occupies four of the top five spots on the list of all-time single-season three-point record holders.
Nothing but net!

Peach baskets were the first basketball hoops.
The ball had to be fished out after each goal scored.
And until the 1950s, the game was played with
a soccer ball. But kicking it was against the rules.

The Boston Celtics are one of the most-respected teams in sports. The Celtics were almost named the Boston Unicorns. How magical!

Wilt Chamberlain is the only player in NBA history to score 100 points in a single game. He's also the only player to get a "double triple-double," which is more than 20 points, rebounds, and assists in a game. *He shoots, he scores!*

In shape for running:
A trip around a baseball diamond is 20 yards longer than a goal-to-goal run on a football field. It just feels like less because it's in a rectangle instead of one long, open run.

Sorry . . . again!
Major League Baseball star
**Richie Ashburn once hit the same fan
with foul balls twice** . . . in the same at-bat.

Can't stop the rhythm . . .
In 1960, **Jimmy Piersall was ejected from a Major League
baseball game for dancing** in centerfield. He was trying
to distract the batter in a close game.

Good luck for his teeth.
Former Major League **pitcher Turk Wendell
had a bit of a crazy superstition.** He brushed
his teeth between innings.

You're outta here!
Baseball umpires don't only have the power
to kick out unruly players. **They also have
the authority to throw out fans** who heckle players.

Talk about a triple play.
A ground-rule double—in which a batter gets to go straight
to second base—is called in baseball if a hit ball bounces
in the outfield and into the stands. **There's also a ground-
rule triple**—a batter takes third base if a fielder tries to
catch a hit ball with his hat.

A **baseball in a big-league ball game doesn't last long.**
It gets replaced after an average of seven pitches.
Or it gets hit out of the park and the crowd goes wild!

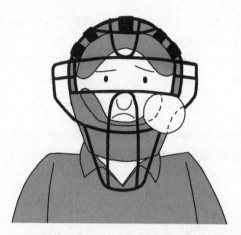

Uh-oh, it's stuck! There's actually a rule in baseball that says what happens if a pitched ball gets stuck in an umpire's protective mask: All runners on base get to move up to the next base.

The baseball rule book dictates what color underwear umpires wear while they're calling a game. They have to wear black in case their pants split open, so the underwear will just blend with the pants.
I see London, I see France, I don't see the umpire's underpants.

The Houston Astros are the only team in Major League Baseball history to go to the World Series as an American League team and then as a National League team. When the Astros were in the NL, they went to the championship in 2005. When they moved to the AL, they won the whole thing in 2017.
That's out of this world!

In Japan, baseball catchers learn how to crouch in a very unique way. Spiked boards are placed on the ground so they won't want to slouch or lose their stance. *Ouch!*

Fastball!
A pitched ball from a big-league pitcher rotates about 15 times on its voyage from pitcher's mound to home plate.

Hey, no fair!
In 1968, **pitcher Bob Gibson of the St. Louis Cardinals was so good**—he won 23 games and struck out 268 batters—that **the next year the league lowered the pitcher's mound by five inches.** That made it easier for batters to hit Gibson's pitches.

Incoming!
Hugh Jennings must have had a baseball magnet inside of him. **The early baseball player was hit by pitches 287 times,** a record that still stands after 100 years.

Babe Ruth was known for hitting home runs.
In 1920, the slugger, by himself, got more home runs than every team in the American League.
That's a lot of dingers!

In 1963, Hall of Fame pitcher Gaylord Perry remarked,
"They'll put a man on the moon before I hit a home run."
On July 20, 1969, a few hours after Neil Armstrong set
foot on the moon, Perry hit the first and only home
run of his career. And he was over the moon!

How very striking!
In 1919, a Major League player named Ray Caldwell
pitched an entire game all the way to two outs in the
ninth inning—**when he was struck by lightning.**
He took a minute to recover and then got the last out.

Not today, sports fans.
**Only two days of the year have no professional
team sports games:** the day before the Major League
Baseball All-Star Game in July . . . and the day after it.

**Green Bay, Wisconsin, is the smallest city with a major pro
sports team**. Only 312,000 people live there.
But they're all big Packers fans.

The sport played by more kids and teenagers worldwide than any other sport: baseball. It's a home run for youth sports!

The Baltimore Ravens are the only sports team named after a poem. The name comes from Edgar Allen Poe's spooky poem "The Raven." Poe lived in Baltimore. Quoth the Raven, "Go Ravens!"

Most NFL teams are owned by a big company or a couple of billionaires, but not the Green Bay Packers.
A group of 112,000 fans (most living locally) all own shares of the team.
By the people, for the people!

The Super Bowl was not as popular at the beginning as it is now. **There's only one known video recording of the first Super Bowl in 1967.** The guy who made it refused to sell it to the NFL.
We'll probably never see it!

Never west to east!
Per the NFL rulebook, **football fields must run in a certain direction**. They always point to the north and to the south.

Only one NFL team has ever gone undefeated:
The 1972 Miami Dolphins won every regular season game, every playoff game, and the Super Bowl.
What a bunch of non-losers!

NFL games take place on Saturdays only late in the season—federal law prohibits them from playing on the same day that college football games are held during that season, and they're on Saturdays.
That would be too much football.

Only one player has ever won every major football award: the Heisman Trophy, a college football national championship, a Super Bowl, MVP of the NFL, and MVP of the Super Bowl. His name is Marcus Allen.
Yeah, he was pretty good at football.

Hit the locker room to hit the books.
The NCAA required college football players to study during halftime until 1925.

Rah, rah, bro boom bah!
Up until World War I, cheerleading was all for guys.
Women stepped in at the college level when most
of the guys went off to war.

What was the first football team to put its logo on its helmets? The Los Angeles Rams. All teams do it now. *Well, except the Cleveland Browns, who just have brownish helmets.*

The shortest-lived NFL team was the Tonawanda Lumbermen.
In 1921, the New York–based team played just one game before it dropped out of the league. (*And they lost the game.*)

New England Patriots star Tom Brady has won five Super Bowls, more than any other quarterback.
Pretty good, considering he was almost completely overlooked in the 2000 NFL Draft—he was the 199th overall pick.
Fortunately, somebody took a chance.

Not only Super Bowl-winning players get Super Bowl rings. The referees who officiate the game get them, too. They're not as big or with as many gems.
But they still make a pretty good souvenir.

It's a rough-and-tumble job.
The average NFL career lasts only 3.3 years.
Running backs are in there for the shortest time, with 2.57 years on average.

Let's go . . . Steagles?!
During World War II, so many players from the NFL's Philadelphia Eagles and Pittsburgh Steelers were off serving in the military that the two teams needed to merge. They were called the Steagles.

Brett Favre is in the Pro Football Hall of Fame, but he played for so long—19 seasons—**that he earned lots of bad records**, like most interceptions thrown (336) and most times sacked (525).
Eh, you win some, you lose some.

The game called soccer in the U.S. is called "football" in England. Teams there are called associations, and the word "soccer" comes from the phrase "association football." *Whew, got all that?*

In 1999 in Bangkok, Thailand, **the largest soccer tournament in history** took place. A whopping 5,098 teams competed.
That must have required a lot of orange slices.

Back and forth, back and forth.
A soccer player does a lot of running throughout a game. In total, it adds up to about six miles.

From "round" the world: 80 percent of all the soccer balls that are made are produced in factories in Pakistan.

In the first modern Olympics in 1896, **Spyridon Belokas of Greece won the bronze medal** in the marathon . . . **but it was revoked when he admitted to secretly hitching a ride on a horse-drawn carriage** during the race. *Cheaters never win!*

Better warm up.
Track and field athletes are more likely to break records late in the day. That's when their body temperatures are at their highest and so they're at peak performance.

Walk, don't run!
Race-walking is an Olympic sport, but what's the difference between walking fast and running? Race-walkers must have one foot on the ground at all times.

It's never too late.
A man named **Ichijirou Araya climbed Mount Fuji . . . at the age of 100.**

The highest-paid athlete in history: probably ancient Roman chariot racer Gaius Appuleius Diocles. He won a total of 35 million sesterces in prize money, which amounts to $15 billion in today's money. *That's a lot of chariot race championships!*

A marathon is 26 miles long. If you ran at literally a snail's pace, it would take you 18 months to finish that marathon. Slow and steady... does not win the race.

Between 1912 and 1948, Olympic events were more than just sports. Medals were awarded for painting, music, and architecture.
Imagine being an Olympic-winning musician!

What are the odds?!
The Kentucky Derby was founded by the grandson of William Clark, half of the Lewis and Clark expedition team.

The village of Llanwrtyd Wells, Wales, holds an event called the "Man vs. Horse Marathon." It's a course of 21.7 miles, and a horse won every year until 2004.
Whoa!

Giddyup!
The phrase "winning hands down" comes from horse racing. It referred to a jockey who won a race without once ever having to pull on the reins.

Olympic swimmer Michael Phelps has personally won more Olympic gold medals than nearly 100 countries. *Talk about heavy metal!*

During the 1930s, speed typing was a popular sport. Go go, type type!

No running!
The 2016 Olympics were held in Rio de Janeiro, Brazil. Under national law, large swimming pools need to have lifeguards present. That means all those swimming events had lifeguards on hand.

No thanks, Olympics.
Denver, Colorado, was picked to host the 1976 Winter Olympics, but then said no when a vote to fund the games failed.
They were held in Austria instead.

From the playground to Olympic glory!
Between 1900 and 1920, **tug-of-war was an official Olympic event.**

And to first place goes the . . . silver medal?
Olympic gold medals are 93 percent silver, 6 percent copper, and just 1 percent actual gold.
The 1912 Olympics were the last time the gold medals were made of solid gold.

The reason there are five Olympic rings is that there are five landmasses where people live: Africa, Europe, Asia, Australia, and the Americas.
Sorry, Antarctica.

The rings on the Olympic flag are red, black, blue, green, and yellow against a white background. That's because the flag of every country on earth includes at least one of those colors.
Everyone is included!

Those colors look great on you!
Pittsburgh is the only American city that has three sports teams that all wear the same team colors.
The Penguins of the NHL, the Pirates of Major League Baseball, and the Steelers of the NFL all sport black and yellow.

Anyone have an eraser?
When the **Boston Bruins of the NHL won the Stanley Cup in 1972,** the team name was etched on the trophy as the "Bqston Bruins."

College and amateur teams from around the U.S. play a sport called underwater hockey. They use 12-inch-long sticks to push a weighted puck around the bottom of a swimming pool.
They use snorkels and occasionally have to come up for air.

Just some goofy trivia.
Skateboarding or surfing with your left foot in the back instead of in the front is called riding "goofy-foot."

Do they still say "king me"?
In England, Checkers is called Draughts.
(It's pronounced "drafts.")

The opposite sides of a die (one of a pair of dice) always add up to seven. Check for yourself!
You're on a "roll" now!

When San Jose was awarded an NHL team, owners asked fans to submit ideas for names. Before they decided on Sharks, one of the finalists was Rubber Puckies.
But it was not *the one!*

The NHL's **Florida Panthers were named to make people aware of endangered species.** The panther is the state animal of Florida, and the team's first owner wanted to make people aware that the animal was threatened. *A purr-fect idea!*

Actual high school sports team mascots:
The Poca H.S. Poca Dots (West Virginia)
and the Abington H.S. Ghosts (Pennsylvania).
Not everybody wants to be the
Wolverines or Wildcats.

You can count them yourself.
The little indentations on a golf ball are called "dimples." The average golf ball has 336 of them.

A hit golf ball can travel very fast. On average, a golf ball tops out at speeds of about 170 miles per hour. Maybe golfers should yell "170!" instead of "Fore!"

Bird is the word.
"Par" is the number of shots a golfer should need to get the ball in the hole. **One under par is called a birdie.** The phrase was created in 1898 by golfer Ab Smith, who had a "bird of a shot" one day.

To get a hole-in-one on a "par five" hole of golf (meaning one that's long or complicated) is very rare. It's only been verified as happening four times. *It's so unlikely it's nicknamed a condor, after the rare bird.*

The **all-time most accomplished left-handed golfer is Phil Mickelson**, who is naturally right-handed. When he was a kid, he learned to golf by mimicking the swing of his left-handed dad. *And then he "left" life as a righty behind!*

Time to celebrate!

In Japan, golfers who hit a hole-in-one are expected to throw a big party for their friends and golf buddies. That's why four million Japanese golfers have hole-in-one insurance—they pay $65 a year, and if they ever get that hole-in-one, they'll get $3,500 to throw the party.

Who's the youngest golfer on record to get a hole-in-one? Coby Orr hit one on a golf course in San Antonio when he was only five years old.
Do they teach golf in kindergarten?

The most expensive golf course in the United States: the Shadow Creek Golf Course in Las Vegas. It costs $500 to play 18 holes. Hey, that's only $28 a hole!

Lots of presidents have played golf, but none more than Woodrow Wilson. He'd play even when there was snow on the ground—using golf balls painted black. *When you gotta play, you gotta play!*

Look out below!
The first outdoor mini-golf courses were built on rooftops in New York City in the 1920s. During the 1930s, Americans could choose from 30,000 courses, including more than 150 rooftop courses in NYC.

Up your alley?
The world's largest bowling alley is in Japan. The Inazawa Bowling Centre opened in 1972 with 116 lanes.

Feeling punchy? In the 19th century, it was common for boxing matches to last up to 100 rounds.

Only two sports have ever been "played" on the moon.
One astronaut hit a golf ball, and another threw
a javelin. And the golf ball is still up there.

**In bowling, getting three strikes in a row is
a rare achievement.** There's even a special term
for it: a turkey.
Gobble-gobble!

**In the late 1950s, Pope John XXIII installed a bowling
alley in the Vatican**, the headquarters of the Catholic
Church.
Did he get a lot of turkeys?

Fuzzy logic?
**Tennis balls are covered in
fuzz to slow them down**, just a little.

Sounds tiring. In 2000, Austrian man Roman Schedler hula-hooped for 71 seconds. That doesn't seem like a long time, but consider that he was doing it with a 53-pound tractor tire.

Can you spare a minute?
The average "last minute" of an NCAA basketball game takes five minutes and 57 seconds to play.

Fill 'er up!
Most NASCAR cars don't use regular air in their tires. They use nitrogen, which makes them race better.

Are we there yet?
The longest NASCAR race is the Coca-Cola 600.
The 600-mile race held at the Charlotte Motor Speedway takes hours to complete.

The longest back-and-forth for a single point in tennis took place in a 1984 women's match. The ball crossed the net 643 times over the course of 29 minutes.
Sounds like they were having a ball.

Let's celebrate! Celebrate what? That there are all of these great facts about holidays—and other special occasions, too—right here, just for you.

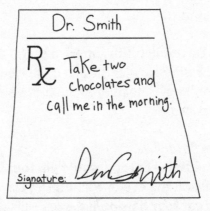

Dr. Smith

Rx Take two chocolates and call me in the morning.

Signature:

Why is chocolate associated with Valentine's Day? In the 1800s, doctors prescribed chocolate to people who were heartbroken, promising it would soothe their pain. Well, it certainly couldn't hurt.

Be mine!
Heart-shaped boxes of chocolates are the bestselling Valentine's Day candy. About 35 million boxes are sold each February.

Write this down (on a piece of candy).
Conversation Hearts, those chalky little candies
with short messages on them, are made by the company
that makes Necco Wafers. **It produces about
eight billion of them, and it takes 11 months to make
them all.**

Valentine's Day is named after St. Valentine.
He was a priest in ancient Rome who married
Christian couples even while the Emperor
was persecuting Christians.
What a love-ly guy!

Valentine's Day took off in America in 1844.
That's when Esther Howland started the New England
Valentine Company. She printed the first Valentine cards.
Candy not included.

The things we do for love.
**Women in medieval Europe would pin four leaves
to their pillow on the eve of Valentine's Day.
Then they'd eat four hardboiled eggs**—including
the shells. It was said that these steps would
make them dream about their future husband.

**In the 18th century, British children went
door-to-door on Valentine's Day.** They'd sing
love songs and beg for cake.
It's never a bad time for cake.

Rice? Who needs rice?
At weddings in medieval England, the guests
threw shoes at the bride and groom.

Too much of a winter wonderland?
**The least popular month for weddings in the U.S.
is January.**
Less than 5 percent of couples "tie the knot" then.

Don't even try unless it's February 14th.
Weddings are not permitted at the Empire State Building.
Ever. Well, **except on Valentine's Day.**

The oldest Valentine in existence was sent in 1415
by France's Duke of Orleans. After being put in
prison in the Tower of London after a battle,
he sent a love letter to his wife. It read: "I am
already sick of love, my very gentle valentine,
since for me you were born too soon, and I for
you was born too late."
What a smooth talker.

Have a heart!
**Red is the color of Valentine's Day because it's the
color of the heart and blood.** For centuries, people
thought feelings of love and romance came from the heart.

**In some parts of Europe in medieval times, wedding
receptions took place in baths.** Guests stood in water
while small toy boats carried food.
Full speed ahead, veggie tray!

Happy birthday to . . . not you.
**In about 3000 B.C., the ancient Egyptians invented
the idea of celebrating birthdays.** But only those
of the queen and male royal family members were celebrated.

**In ancient Greece, the birthdays of all
adult males were celebrated.** Women's and
children's birthdays were not observed.
Pass the party hat to your dad, please.

The odds that you, a parent, and a grandparent will all have the same birthday? Very low—about 1 in 160,000.
Happy birthday, happy birthday, happy birthday!

Happy Hedgehog Day!
Groundhog Day is based on an old German holiday called Candlemas, except that they used a hedgehog.
When German settlers came to the U.S., they brought the holiday but went with groundhogs, which were more plentiful.

They had wedding cakes in ancient Rome. Guests wished the bride good luck by smashing the cake over her head. Why would they do that to a perfectly good cake?

Sounds pretty fishy... The French call April 1 *Poisson d'Avril*, or "April Fish." French children sometimes prank their friends by taping a picture of a fish onto their back.

St. Patrick's Day as it's celebrated today began in the United States in the late 19th and early 20th centuries.
Large numbers of newly arrived Irish immigrants set the day aside to celebrate their heritage and their homeland. *How lucky for us!*

What day is it?!
Some say **April Fools' Day started in the 1500s with a calendar switch**—from the Julian calendar (with the new year starting in March) to the Gregorian calendar (which starts on January 1). People were made fun of if they didn't know about the switch and followed the old calendar.

Couldn't you just dye?
The most popular color to dye eggs is blue.
After that come purple, and then pink.

We 're over the moon! Why does Easter take place on
a different day every year? It's set for the first
Sunday after the first full moon of the spring.
The earliest that can happen is March 22, and
the latest is April 25.

A little cherry in your eggs?
**Egg-dying has been an Easter activity since long before
artificial dyes were invented.** Among the natural dyes
used: cherry juice for red eggs, carrots for yellow ones,
and red onion skins for purple.

Watch it!
About 87 percent of American parents fill Easter baskets for their kids. Then 81 percent of those parents proceed to steal candy out of them.

Americans didn't know about the Easter Bunny until the late 1600s. Dutch immigrants who settled in Pennsylvania brought the idea to the New World. *Thank you very Dutch!*

Ain't no bunny!
In Switzerland, they don't have an Easter Bunny making deliveries. They have an **Easter Cuckoo.**

King of the Easter Bunnies?
In 1307, King Edward I of England asked his kitchen staff **to boil 450 eggs. Then he had them covered in gold leaf** and gave them all away to his servants.

How egg-citing!
In Haux, France, they follow Easter Sunday with Easter Monday. They cook a **gigantic omelette for 1,000 people**—made with about 5,000 eggs.

Kids love getting Easter baskets filled with treat-stuffed plastic eggs. For a kid named Kyle Johnson, the eggs are enough. In 2012, **he set a world record by holding 14 plastic eggs in one hand.** *Eggs-cellent!*

On Easter Monday in Hungary, some people engage in a tradition called "sprinkling." Guys dump a bucket of water on a girl they like and ask them for a kiss. They probably won't get one if they do something like that!

They should have a statewide Easter egg hunt!

In Spain, Easter is often called the Feast of Flowers, or *Pascua Florida*. When Spanish explorer Juan Ponce de Leon "discovered" a part of North America on Easter Sunday 1512, **he named the land Florida.**

In 2007, at Cypress Gardens Adventure Park in Winter Haven, Florida, **the biggest Easter egg hunt in history** took place. Almost 10,000 kids searched for 501,000 eggs.
And you just know they found every last one of them.

According to a legend in Finland, Easter is when witches roam the earth. So kids there have fun with it—they smear dirt on their faces, wrap scarves around their heads, and carry brooms.
Sounds more like Halloween than Easter!

Ann Jarvis was a Civil War nurse who helped heal the nation after that conflict by encouraging people to reach out to their mothers with **Mother's Friendship Day**. When she died in 1905, her daughter, Anna Jarvis, received hundreds of cards from people whose lives were touched by her mother, so she started celebrating it in 1908 in West Virginia. **Mother's Day became a national holiday in 1914.**
And the number of cards multiplied!

Dad fact!
**Father's Day started as a local holiday
in Spokane, Washington, in 1910.** It spread around
the country but didn't become a permanent national
holiday until Richard Nixon signed a bill in 1972.

Say uncle! Say uncle!
You've heard of Mother's Day, and Father's Day,
and Grandparents' Day, but did you know
the last Friday of July is Aunt and Uncle's Day?

Why is Flag Day a thing? June 14 commemorates
the day in 1777 that the "stars and stripes" was officially
adopted as a symbol of the U.S.A. by the Second
Continental Congress.
It was a banner day!

There was a fourth of July before then, but it wasn't
the "Fourth of July" until 1781. That's when **Massachusetts
became the first state to make Independence Day
a holiday.** It became a nationally observed one in 1870.
Did a nationwide cookout break out?!

There are thousands of fireworks displays across
the country on the Fourth of July. **The biggest: Macy's
Fourth of July Fireworks Show in New York City.**
The celebration includes 400,000 rockets launched at
a rate of 1,000 per second from six floating barges.
BOOM!

When Alaska and Hawaii became the 49th and 50th states in 1959, a nationwide contest was held to design a new flag—the field of stars had to be updated. The winner: Robert Heft, who came up with his idea as a school project. His teacher gave him a B-minus, but when his design was selected as the winner, the grade was changed to an A. Extra credit?

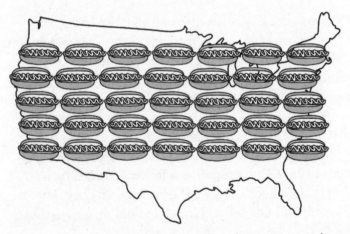

At cookouts across the country, Americans eat a total of 150 million hot dogs every Fourth of July. That's enough to stretch from coast to coast five times over!

Know any good ones?
The only month without a major holiday: August.
However, August 16 is National Tell a Joke Day.

Halloween by any other name . . .
In England, **jack o' lanterns are sometimes called spunkies.**

Spooktacular!
In parts of Iowa, **kids knock on doors on Halloween** but they don't say "trick or treat." **They say "tricks for treats."** Before they get a piece of candy, they have to tell a silly joke.

Ready to visit the turnip patch?
Carving jack o' lanterns came to America with immigrants from Great Britain. Pumpkins are used, because they're a very common vegetable in the U.S. They weren't common in the British Isles, where they used turnips and beets.

A lot of Halloween traditions come from an ancient Irish holiday called Samhain (pronounced "sow-wen"). One Irish Halloween activity: snap-apple. An apple is tied to a doorframe with string and kids try to bite it. *It's like bobbing for apples while standing up!*

One Samhain tradition that stayed in Ireland: **barmback.** It's a fruitcake stuffed with wrapped trinkets that "predict your future" for the months ahead. **If you get a ring in your piece, it means you'll find love. A coin means you'll get rich.** *And at any rate, you get cake!*

Trick or treat, smell my feet . . . November 11 is St. Martin's Day in Belgium and the Netherlands. **Kids celebrate by making paper lanterns and knocking on doors in search of candy.** But instead of saying "trick or treat," they recite poems.

The first Macy's Thanksgiving Day Parade was held in New York City in 1924. There were no giant balloons quite yet, but it did feature a lot of animals from the Central Park Zoo. *And for that, we're thankful.*

The first big balloon was introduced into the Macy's Thanksgiving Day Parade in 1927. It was the cartoon character Felix the Cat. *Purrrrrfect!*

No giant balloons were allowed in the Macy's Thanksgiving Day Parade in 1928, 1929, or 1930. Why not? During its first parade in 1927, the Felix balloon got caught in telephone wires . . . and burst into flames. *Not so hot.*

The biggest pumpkin ever: it was 2,624.6 pounds, grown by Mathias Willemijns of Belgium. That's as big as a car!

Not even Superman could save the day.
The 1986 Macy's Thanksgiving Day Parade was a disaster. It was so windy that one balloon knocked over a lamppost, another had its arm ripped off, and a tree ripped off the Superman balloon's hand.

You are getting very sleepy...Some people call that sleepy, extra-full feeling after Thanksgiving dinner a "food coma." The scientific name for it is *postprandial somnolence.*

Be sure to save room for pumpkin pie!
Americans eat a total of 10 million *tons* of turkey each and every Thanksgiving.

Thanksgiving used to be held one week later. In 1939, President Franklin D. Roosevelt moved it up a week. That way the Christmas shopping season could get off to an earlier start.
Happy holidays!

To purchase all of the birds used in "The 12 Days of Christmas," it would cost you about $1.3 million.
That's a lot of turtledoves.

Ever hear about "sugarplums" in old Christmas stories?
What is a sugarplum, anyway? It's chopped dried fruit,
nuts, and spices rolled into a ball
and covered with sugar.

Did someone say cake?
Fruitcake is a classic holiday treat. Most of them are made in Claxton, Georgia, the "fruitcake capital of the world."
Bakeries there make 4 million pounds of fruitcake every year.

Now that's a Christmas gift!
Author Robert Louis Stevenson (who wrote *Treasure Island*) **left his November birthday in his will** to a friend who had been born on Christmas and didn't like it.

The first-ever text message was sent on December 3, 1990. The message said, "Merry Christmas!" *Cool technology, but a little early.*

O Christmas goose!
Today, artificial Christmas trees are made of plastic.
The first ones, made in Germany in the 1800s,
were made out of goose feathers dyed green.

Are Santa's reindeer male or female? They are often
portrayed as having antlers. Because male reindeer shed
their antlers in early December and females have thin antlers
through the winter, that means Santa's reindeers are
all ladies.
Girl squad!

Not so minty fresh.
Among the weirder flavors of candy canes available
during the holidays: gravy, bacon, hot sauce, and pickle.

In "The 12 Days of Christmas" song, one of the gifts
is a turtledove. It gets its name from the Latin word
turtur, or dove. That means they're actually called
dove-doves. Wait, can you repeat that?!

Who put on the tree topper?!
According to *Guinness World Records*, **the tallest Christmas tree of all time was a 221-foot Douglas fir.**
It went on display in 1950 at the Northgate Shopping Center in Seattle.

Christmas trees are teenagers!
How long does it take to grow a Christmas tree?
The average one sold is about 15 years old.

Not just for Halloween. In Poland, spider webs are a Christmas tree decoration. Spiders are a symbol of goodness and wealth there.

A lot of American kids, and especially kids in Europe, **always get an orange or a tangerine in their Christmas stocking**. That tradition comes from **nuns in the 12th century who left a sock full of nuts and fruit** at the homes of the less fortunate.
We assume the socks weren't used.

Christmas surprise.
According to a central European folk tale, **children who are born on Christmas will grow up to become either lawyers or criminals.**

It wasn't always a holiday?
The first state to officially make Christmas a holiday was Alabama, in 1836. It wasn't a national holiday until 1870.

Mistletoe—the plant that calls for a kiss when you're standing under it with someone—**gets its name from the Old English word *misteltan*, which means "little dung twig**." The plant's seeds are spread by birds that eat the plant and then leave their waste . . . with the seeds still in it.
How romantic!

No tree shall stand!
President Teddy Roosevelt was an environmentalist who wanted to protect nature. For that reason, **he wouldn't allow a Christmas tree in the White House.**

Legos have been one of the most popular toys in the world for more than 40 years. **During the holiday shopping season, 28 sets of Legos are sold every second.** *That's really building something.*

In France, Santa Claus is called Père Noël, or "Father Christmas." Kids set out their shoes and leave cookies for him and carrots for the reindeer. Père Noël returns the favor by filling the shoes with candy. Mmm, shoe candy!

If the 1970 TV special *Santa Claus Is Coming to Town* were to be believed, **Mrs. Claus's first name is Jessica.** *So it's not "Mrs."?*

Just hanging around . . .
In medieval times, actors would perform Christmas plays
about Adam and Eve and would hang apples on trees.
**That brought about the idea of decorating a tree
at Christmas.**

**On Christmas in Japan, it's traditional to eat
Kentucky Fried Chicken**. Families reserve a table
and make their orders months in advance.
What are you, chicken?

**When NASA launched the *Voyager* space probe
in 1977,** engineers made sure they set the spacecraft's
trajectory **to avoid any potential collisions with
Santa's sleigh** at Christmas.
Thanks, NASA!

Ho! ho! ho!
The Christmas carol "Up on the Housetop" was written
in 1864. It mentions "Old St. Nick" delivering presents,
making it **the first Christmas song to mention
Santa Claus.**

Always get a second opinion.
Songwriters Jay Livingston and Ray Evans called their
Christmas song "Tinkle Bell," until Livingston's wife pointed
out that most people associate the word "tinkle" with going
to the bathroom.
That's when they changed it to "Silver Bells."

Because it's in the Southern Hemisphere, Australian seasons are opposite to North America's. That means Christmas falls right in the middle of summer. Kids don't leave out milk and cookies Down Under—they leave Santa a glass of lemonade. Still enough sugar to fuel his travels!

Where it's Christmas every day!
There are more than **140 towns and cities in the United States with "Christmas" in their names.**

Christmas trees originated in Germany. They were introduced to the United States when German troops came to assist the colonists in the Revolutionary War in the late 1700s.
Danke schön! (That means "Thank you" in German.)

During Christmas in the Canadian province of Newfoundland, **people called Mummers dress up in costumes. Then they go from house to house dancing**, playing music, and trying to get people to guess their true identities. *The great Christmas mystery!*

In 1917, **a boat full of explosives blew up in the docks of the city of Halifax, Nova Scotia, Canada.** The city of Boston sent so many people and supplies that as a thank-you, **the Nova Scotia government still sends Boston its official Christmas tree every year**. *That's what the holidays are all about.*

Sounds like it would go better with a certain October holiday. In the 1800s, **it was a Christmas Eve tradition in the U.S. and England to tell ghost stories**.

X marks the holiday. **Why is Christmas abbreviated to Xmas?** X is the Greek letter *chi*, which in Greek is also an abbreviation for "Christ." X + mas = Christmas.

Tough or easy spelling test? **There are at least 16 ways to spell Hanukkah** that are technically correct. Because Hanukkah is transliterated from Hebrew letters, there is not an obvious English spelling. The most common are "Hanukkah" and "Chanukah."

That's lit!

The running of the torch isn't reserved for just the Olympics. During Hanukkah in Israel, runners race a burning torch about 20 miles from the Israeli city of Modiin to Jerusalem. The chief rabbi then lights a giant menorah at the Western Wall. Other Jewish communities around the world have joined in similar celebrations.

Our heads are spinning . . .

Major League Dreidel is a real thing. It's a New York City–based association of hard-core dreidel players. Hundreds of people take part in their tournament each year.

Feels like Fryday . . .

Why are fried foods so popular during Hanukkah? Oil is celebrated to remember the miracle of the one day's worth of lamp oil that lasted for eight days.

Say cheese!

The fried-potato pancakes called latkes that are a popular food during Hanukkah didn't start as potatoes. They only became part of the recipe as potatoes became common and less expensive than cheese, which latkes were made from earlier.

A delicious wonder of the world:
On the first night of Hanukkah in 1997, **a 12-foot-high pyramid of 6,400 jelly doughnuts** (traditional treats called "soufganiyot") was built near the Israeli town of Afula.

52 years young!
Founded in 1966, Kwanzaa is a celebration of African community, family, and culture that begins December 26 and lasts for seven days.

Five, four, three, two, one . . . Happy New Year!
Each New Year's Eve, **a giant ball drops in New York's Times Square** to ring in the new year. **That ball is called the Star of Hope.**

A New Year's Eve tradition in South America: wearing brightly colored underwear. Legend holds that if you want to get rich in the new year, you should wear yellow ones. If you're looking for love, wear red ones. Hey, why not both?

It's a New Year's Eve tradition in the Philippines for kids to jump up and down 12 times at midnight. Old folk wisdom says it will increase their chances of getting taller in the new year.

Heavy metal!
On New Year's Eve in Germany and Finland, people predict the future by melting lead. They pour hot, liquid lead into water, where it solidifies into a shape. If a heart or ring forms, the person will get married in the new year. If the lead clump looks like a pig, it means you'll never be hungry.

In large quantities, such as in a sugar factory,
sugar dust can ignite and explode.
Talk about a candy crush!

A sweet fact:
A lot of people think that eating too much sugar makes kids hyper. There's actually no scientific evidence that this is true.
But everything in balance—it can have other unhealthy effects.

A sugar rush from fruit?
Dates are the sweetest fruit. They have the highest
concentration of sugar, at 55 percent.

The variety of **banana sold almost everywhere is
called the Cavendish**. Before that was a now-extinct
kind called the Gros Michel, which tasted more like
how banana candy tastes today.
Doesn't sound very "gros" at all.

These bananas are bananas!
There's a type of **banana called the burro that's
rectangular and tastes like lemons**. Another type, called
the ice cream banana, is creamy and has blue skin.

A berry weird fact to know:
Strawberries aren't technically berries.
But avocados, pumpkins, tomatoes, watermelons, and
bananas are.

The seed of knowledge:
All those little white things on the outside of a strawberry are seeds. How many? **The average strawberry is dotted with about 200 seeds.**

It certainly doesn't taste like it.
Despite being very sour, lemons are loaded with sugar.
They've got more of the sweet stuff
than strawberries.

After Coke and Pepsi, **what's the #3 bestselling soda in the world?** Orange-flavored Fanta.
A toast to Fanta!

Brown food coloring is added to Coca-Cola.
If it weren't, Coke would be a weird shade of green.
Does that mean it counts as a vegetable?

When it was first sold in 1886,
Coca-Cola was sold as a headache remedy.
Caffeine does help headaches, so they weren't totally lying.

Cheap thrills:
**The price of a bottle of Coca-Cola in 1886
was just five cents**. The price didn't go up to 10 cents
until 1960.

Root beer was first an herbal tea made up
of more than two dozen herbs, roots, and berries.
Then inventor Charles Hires added the mixture,
and some sugar, to carbonated water.
And that's the "root" of all sodas.

*No burger necessary.
The number-one bestselling food across all
restaurants in the United States: French fries.*

Potatoes are part of many different European cultures' cuisines, but they originate in Peru. They were brought back to Europe by explorers who visited the South American country in the 1500s.
Spudtastic!

Pleased to meat you?
A beef cow weighs several hundred pounds,
but not very much of it is usable meat. The average cow is good for 400 quarter-pound hamburger patties.

Go with the flow! **Ketchup leaves its bottle at a rate of 25 miles per year.**
Your fries might be cold by then.

There are medicinal uses for onions. Doctors say chewing a raw one can clear up a stuffy nose.
No thanks.

If black pepper gets in your nose, it can make you sneeze.
That's because of a chemical in it called piperine.
And now you nose.

You're barking up the right tree.
The parts of most plants we eat are the leaves, berries, or roots—but **it's the bark of the cinnamon tree that's used to make cinnamon.**

What's up, doc?
The spices anise, fennel, dill, caraway, coriander, and cumin are all technically vegetables. They're closely related to the carrot.

Catch a wave!
The microwave was invented by accident. A scientist working in a research lab walked by a radar tube and the heat coming off it melted the chocolate bar in his pocket.

Now that's a hot one: You could technically cook an egg on a sidewalk on a hot day. But to cook it fully, the surface temperature of the sidewalk would have to be at least 158° Fahrenheit.

Pencils were invented long before pencil erasers were.
People used breadcrumbs to rub out mistakes.
A delicious error!

The very first microwave oven hit stores in 1947.
It was called the Radarange and cost $3,000,
which works out to about $30,000 in today's money.
That's one expensive meal.

May the odds be not in your favor.
If you drop a buttered piece of toast, odds are
you'll drop the butter side onto the floor. There's
a 62 percent chance of that happening.

A traditional breakfast in Wales consists of bacon, clams, and seaweed paste on toast. Suddenly, cereal doesn't sound so bad.

Oui!
Think croissants are one of the most "French" foods out there? The buttery pastry actually originated in Austria. In the 1700s, Marie Antoinette of Austria became queen of France and introduced the pastry to her new country.

In Tibet, the **traditional drink is a tea made out of salted yak butter** that's gone bad. *Suddenly, coffee doesn't sound so bad.*

Cap'n Crunch has a first name.
The cereal mascot's full name is Horatio Magellan Crunch.
Pleased to eat you!

Would he like some eggs with that?
A man named Matt Stone set the world record in bacon-eating. He devoured 182 slices in just five minutes.

The best part of waking up?
Every day, Americans eat about 175
million eggs and 4 million pounds of bacon.
Now that's a big breakfast.

To grow the orange trees that will make orange juice requires a lot of water. **It takes about 50 glasses of water to raise the oranges to make one glass's worth of orange juice.**
Orange you glad you read this?

It takes a lot of sap to make maple syrup.
Fifty gallons of raw sap produce just one gallon
of maple syrup.
Along with a lot of sugar.

Moos you can use:
Ever wonder how many squirts of a cow's udder
it takes to make a gallon of milk? About 350.

French toast isn't called "French toast" everywhere.
It's also called German toast, American toast,
Spanish toast, nun's toast, cream toast, amarilla,
Bombay toast, and the Poor Knights of Windsor.
How eggs-citing!

The "lolli" part of the word "lollipop" comes from lolly,
an Old English word. It means "tongue."
Hope this one "sticks" in your brain.

Pucker up: **Hershey's Kisses got their name** because the machine that makes them looks like it's kissing the conveyor belt.
And it was true love.

The "M and M" in M&Ms stand for the names of the candy's creators. They were Forrest Mars and Bruce Murrie.
Mmmm-hmm!

M&Ms were invented for soldiers to have chocolate that was easy to transport and didn't melt.
The candy shell prevents it from melting in pockets.
They do "melt in your mouth, not in your hand," after all.

The French word for the kiwi fruit is *sours végétales*.
It means "vegetable mice."
Yummy!

Here's one to chew on....
Bubblegum was first available in 1906. It was sold
under the name Blibber-Blubber.

Where are the other musketeers?
The Three Musketeers candy bar consists of
chocolate-covered, whipped, chocolate-flavored nougat.
It got its name because it used to come three flavors
to one package: chocolate, vanilla, and strawberry.

Candy from space?
Sour Patch Kids were invented in the 1970s in Canada
during a time when there were a lot of UFO sightings.
They were originally named Mars Men.

A Hershey **chocolate bar is made up of 12 individual rectangles of chocolate called "pips."**
When you have one, you always want s'more.

Heads up!
Kids love PEZ Dispensers.
They get loaded up with candy flavors like orange, cherry, and strawberry. But some flavors that flopped: mint, eucalyptus, and yogurt.

It's named for a horse, of course!
Snickers got its name from a racehorse.
That was what a thoroughbred owned by the candy's maker was called.

C is for koekje?
The English word "cookie" comes from the Dutch word *koekje,* which means "small cake."

Where do we go to get the other 0.22?
A scientific study found that **Double Stuff Oreos actually have only 1.78 times the crème filling** as regular Oreos.

There's no "cream" in the "crème."
Oreos contain no dairy products whatsoever.
They're actually vegan, meaning they contain no animal-based ingredients at all.

Most popular sandwich to pack in kids' lunches?
Peanut butter and jelly.
Why mess with a classic?

A full one-third of all peanuts grown in the U.S.
will eventually **get turned into peanut butter**.
And most of that will wind up in peanut butter sandwiches.

This fact is nuts!
California leads the world in almond production.
This one state grows over half the world's total supply.

Feel the heat.
The smaller the pepper, the hotter it is.
Color has nothing to do with it.

You will learn an interesting fact

Fortune cookies are made by flattening the dough into circles and baking them. They're taken out of the oven while still soft, and then a fortune slip is placed inside each before the cookies are shaped and harden naturally.

If you see a green turnip, that doesn't mean it's underripe. **It's actually sunburned.**
Should've worn sunscreen!

An explosive fact:
Dynamite is made up of many ingredients.
One of them is a trace amount of peanuts.

New Mexico has two official state vegetables. They're chiles and frijoles (pinto beans, which are legumes—not vegetables).
Eat your veggies . . . and legumes.

Cucumbers are a fruit, not a vegetable.
They also have the least nutrition of any fruit.
The one with the most: avocado.
Pass the guac!

Americans eat a lot of pizza.
Every day, the country put together eats 18 acres worth.
That's not even counting the breadsticks.

Hold the pepperoni.
Pizza is popular around the world,
but **different countries prefer different toppings.**
In Chile, the most popular ones are clams and mussels.

Calzone is a popular dish at Italian restaurants.
It was invented in Canada, at a Chinese restaurant.
It's been all over the world!

Stop and smell the barbecue!
In a poll to determine the "most American" scent,
the winner, with 39 percent, was the smell of
barbecued meat cooking on a grill.

Compliments to the chef:
In some parts of the Middle East, it's okay to burp
at the dinner table. It's considered a compliment
to the cook.

There are thousands and thousands of restaurants
in New York City. So many, in fact, that
a person could **eat out every night of their life in NYC
and never dine at the same place twice**.
Bon apétit!

The first fast-food kids' meal was introduced in 1973
at a now-closed chain called Burger Chef. It offered
kid-sized portions of a burger and fries with a soft drink.
And of course, it included a free toy.

The first fast-food drive-through was installed in the 1950s. Red's Giant Hamburg in Springfield, Illinois, installed a "service window."
It used to be a gas station!

Canned fact: There's no such fish as a sardine. Sardines are herring, but the canning process that makes them possible was invented in Sardinia, Italy.

Flamin' Hot Cheetos were invented by a janitor who worked at the Cheetos factory.
He got a promotion to the marketing team.

They'll feed you, but you've got to bring your own utensils.
In medieval England, you were expected to bring your own knife if you were invited to dinner at somebody's house.

Can you hear me now?
An ear of corn consists of corn kernels and strands of corn silk. **There's one piece of corn silk for every kernel.**

Don't try this at Thanksgiving dinner!
When cranberries are ripe, they will bounce like rubber balls. In fact, growers use this simple test to see if a berry is good.

This one is pretty corny.... Corn is used to make high fructose corn syrup, a common food sweetener. One bushel of corn contains enough sweetness to make about 400 cans of soda.

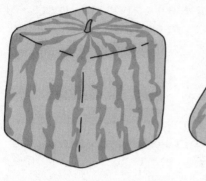
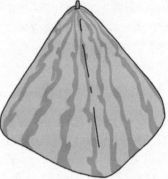

In Japan, farmers grow watermelons in special
containers. They make the final product come
out in shapes like pyramids or cubes.
That's how to make fruit fun.

Just plum crazy!
In 1984, **Alan Newbold set a record when he ate
150 prunes**, or dried plums, in 31 seconds.

That's why they bob. . . .
Apples are somewhere between 18 and 25 percent air.
So floating comes naturally.

Want to monkey around?
The next time a friend asks you for help by asking for
"a hand," have some fun and hand him some bananas.
A bunch of bananas is called a hand.

Very ap-peeling:
Bananas debuted in the U.S. at the
1876 Philadelphia World's Fair. They cost 10 cents
apiece, which is the equivalent of about $2 today.

Take your pick: The apples you buy at a supermarket
probably aren't that fresh. They might have
been harvested as long as a year ago.

Belgian waffles aren't from Belgium.
A waffle vendor at the 1964 New York World's Fair
added yeast to waffle batter to make them fluffier
and called them that so they'd sound exotic.
Hey, works for us.

French fries aren't from France—they originated in Belgium, where lots of people speak French. The name refers to how they're cut—long strips are called "French" style.
Whatever the reason, they're still delicious.

Christopher Columbus introduced a lot of European foods to the Americas. Some of these were onions, wheat, barley, olives, lettuce, and garlic.
So that's why there aren't any vampires in North America!

All you can eat!
The first Chinese restaurant in the U.S. was a San Francisco buffet in 1849 called Macao and Woosung. It cost $1.

First pizza delivery: **In 1889, the owner of a Naples, Italy, pizza parlor** named Raffaele Esposito delivered a pie to a home where the king and queen of Italy were staying.
We hope he got a nice tip.

Durian is a southeast Asian fruit that looks like a grenade and smells like dirty socks. It's apparently delicious, despite its green prickly skin.
We'll pass.

No foods are naturally blue, even blueberries. They're actually purple.
Now we've got the blues.

Here's some cold comfort:
The average person uses 3.2 ice cubes
when they want ice in their drink.

But can you write on a blackboard with it?
Spinach has a chalky aftertaste. That's because it's
high in a type of calcium that's used to make chalk.

Camels produce milk, and humans can drink it.
It never curdles.
One lump or two?

Cheesy does it.
**France is one of the world's biggest consumers
and exporters of cheese**. In fact, more than half
of all the different varieties of cheese were first
created in France.

Out-of-this-world mac 'n' cheese is easy!
Macaroni and cheese is an astronaut favorite.
And it's easier to cook in space than on Earth:
Just add water, let it sit for 10 minutes, and you're done.

Way beyond pasketti . . .
There are more than **600 different shapes of pasta**
produced worldwide.

Soup's on!
In 2010, archaeologists found a bowl of soup
in a tomb in China. It was 2,400 years old and still liquid.

Got glue?
In cereal commercials, they don't use actual milk
for the milk. Instead, the ad makers use white glue,
because it glistens under bright lights.

Some fat-free salad dressings have an extra ingredient. The fat taken out has to be replaced with something to make them creamy, so food makers use titanium dioxide, which also makes sunscreen seem creamy.
Yum?

Every four seconds, **somebody somewhere in the world opens and eats from a can of Spam.**
Talk about a can-do attitude!

According to a recent poll, the **most hated foods among Americans** are: 1. tofu, 2. liver, and 3. yogurt.
So no seconds on that tofu-liver-yogurt casserole then?

We all scream for ice cream facts!
The top three bestselling ice cream flavors in the U.S. are vanilla, chocolate, and surprisingly, butter pecan.

Jell-O has tried out a lot of weird flavors over the years. Some that totally flopped: celery, coffee, cola, apple, and chocolate.
There's always room for Jell-O, except for those flavors.

The most popular candy in the United States
that isn't made of chocolate: LifeSavers.
They're on a roll!

This fact rocks!
There's only **one rock that humans can and do eat.**
It's salt.

A very sweet problem to have.
In 1981, **food company Nabisco bought the Curtiss
Candy Company**, maker of the Butterfinger candy bar.
Somebody misplaced the recipe, so workers had to
come up with a whole new way to make them.

8
ALL AROUND THE WORLD

We searched all over the globe to find you these facts about people, places, and cultures.

Say it ain't snow! Snow days are rare worldwide. An estimated two-thirds of the entire world population has never seen snow.

With temperatures dipping to minus 96° Fahrenheit, **Oymyakon, Siberia, is the coldest place on the planet.** Your breath can even freeze and hang in the air. *Hope you brushed your teeth!*

Look out below, eventually!
In a tropical rain forest, there are so many trees and leaves to navigate that it can take a falling raindrop more than 10 minutes to hit the ground.

Here's a fact that's been rumbling around for a while. **There are no thunderstorms at the North Pole or the South Pole.** It's because there isn't enough warm air there.

Iceland is cold, but it's not covered in ice. In the Icelandic language, Iceland means "island." *Icy what they did there!*

Inuit people who live in Canada near the North Pole have to **store their food in refrigerators**. *Why is that odd?* It's so cold that **if they left the food out, it would freeze.**

Giant floating popsicles!
Not all icebergs are white.
Some are green, some are black, and some are blue.

Today's weather: never-ending storms. At any given moment, there are about 1,800 thunderstorms going on somewhere in the atmosphere.

It's about time somebody dusted!
Every year, the world's deserts whip up a lot of dust.
In all, about 1.7 billion metric tons of the stuff.

The largest desert in the world: Antarctica. It has no permanent residents, but about 1,000 researchers live there at any one time.
They should call Antarctica Down Under instead of Australia!

The Dead Sea is technically a lake. It's called "dead" because the salt content is so high that fish can't survive in it.
Any pepper, though?

A hotel in Bolivia is made entirely of salt. Even the furniture is made out of salt.
Bring some pretzels for dipping!

A hard shell to crack.
The *charango* is the national instrument of Bolivia. It's traditionally made from armadillo shells.

Ah, we love you, too, Australia!
There's a massive, heart-shaped coral reef that lives off the coast of Australia.

More wild camels live in Australia than anywhere else. It's "hump day" every day!

Asia is the largest continent, and Australia is the smallest. You could fit six Australias inside of one Asia. *Crikey!*

What's your name?
England, Great Britain, and the United Kingdom are not the same thing. Great Britain is the name of the island that holds England, Scotland, and Wales, which together, along with Northern Ireland, make up a country called the United Kingdom of Great Britain and Northern Ireland, or U.K. for short.

France isn't really called France. Technically, its name is the French Republic.
Pass the French Republic fries.

Bank on this.
The Bank of England was founded by a Scotsman.
The Bank of Scotland was founded by an Englishman.

That's the state of things.
Before it was a state, **Hawaii** was independent.
It's the only state that was once a kingdom.

Bangkok is the capital of Thailand. **That's just a nickname—Bangkok's full name is** Krung Thep Mahanakhon Amon Rattanakosin Mahinthara Ayuthaya Mahadilok Phop Noppharat Ratchathani Burirom Udomratchaniwet Mahasathan Amon Piman Awatan Sathit Sakkathattiya Witsanukam Prasit, which means "City of angels, great city of immortals, magnificent city of the nine gems, seat of the king, city of royal palaces, home of gods incarnate, erected by Vishvakarman at Indra's behest."
Now repeat that back.

In Chongqing, China, there are special lanes on the sidewalk for phone users to walk in so they don't bump into non-texters. But watch out for those fountains!

The Beijing Duck in China is **the largest restaurant in the world**. It can seat 9,000 people.
Don't get lost on the way to the bathroom!

Casa Botín in Madrid, Spain, is the oldest restaurant in the world. It opened in 1725.
That's a long time to wait for a table.

The biggest mall on the planet is the Mall of America in Minnesota. It's so big that it could comfortably store 258 Statues of Liberty.
And Lady Liberty can shop for a new torch while she's there.

Ready for an evening of international entertainment?
The Haskell Opera House sits right on the U.S./Canadian border. The stage is in Quebec, while the audience's seats are in Vermont.

Let's go to the park!
New York's Central Park is larger than two entire nations: Monaco and Vatican City.

Start your engines!
Vatican City could fit entirely inside the Indianapolis Motor Speedway. That's where the Indy 500 is held each year.

Are they on your list?
The top countries visited by tourists worldwide are France and Spain. The United States is number three.

Take your pick! The Statue of Liberty's nose is about the size of a kid. It's four feet, six inches long.

Afraid of heights?
The Statue of Liberty is pretty tall, but it's not as tall as **the Eiffel Tower.** The Paris landmark **is taller than three Statue of Liberties and three school buses put together.**

Howdy!
There's an Eiffel Tower in Paris, France, and a smaller Eiffel Tower in Paris, Texas.
That one has a huge cowboy hat on top.

There's a real town called Difficult, Tennessee.
It was named that when the settlers couldn't agree on a better name.
What a difficult situation!

There are four American towns called Peanut.
They're in the states of California, Pennsylvania,
Tennessee, and West Virginia.
That's a little nutty!

There's an actual city called Boring, Oregon.
Its sister city: Dull, Scotland.
Yawn.

Hove Mobile Park City in North Dakota is the smallest official town in the United States. It has a population of two.
Which means they've each got a 50 percent chance at being mayor!

Hello, down there!
More than 90 percent of the earth's population lives above the equator, in countries in the Northern Hemisphere.

The number of people living in cities surpassed the number of people living in the country for the first time in May 2007.
Welcome to the city, everybody.

Each second the world's population increases by 2.4 people. That's 86,000 new people every day.
Happy birthday!

The most commonly spoken language in the world is Mandarin Chinese. More than 815 million people speak it.
How do you say "that's a lot" in Mandarin?

In Korea, saying "I love you" isn't that popular. Instead, sweeties tell each other a phrase that means "You are the bee of my flower."
Oh, honey!

Never write a note in red ink in Portugal. It's considered rude.
Why, I never!

That's barely enough to get going on a video game!
In Japan, summer vacation is much shorter than it is in the U.S. Kids there only get six weeks.

A dog-lover's dream?
There are more pets than there are children in all of Japan.

Think of green as a lucky color?
In Scotland, it's bad luck for
anyone to wear green to a wedding.

It's a common practice in Ghana to name babies
after the day of the week on which they're born.
Thank God it's Kofi!

Just one more reason to avoid it!
Dying is illegal in the Norwegian town of Longyearbyen.

When it opened in 1931, **the Empire State Building**
in New York City was the tallest structure on earth.
It took 10 million bricks to construct it.
That's how you build an empire, brick by brick.

Which is bigger, **Walt Disney World in Florida**
or the city of San Francisco? They're about the same size.
Yes, but San Francisco doesn't have any rides!

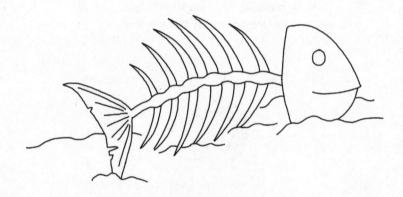

Forget "burying the hatchet"!
It's considered a good luck charm in Tunisia to bury
fish bones in a new building's foundation.

Parked on the sofa or in the garage?
A two-car garage in the U.S. is larger than
the average home in Tokyo, Japan.

Well, that's one way to recycle.
There's a bike path connecting the Dutch towns of
Leeuwarden and Stien. **The asphalt is mixed with toilet
paper that was filtered out of local sewage systems.**

This one really sticks!
Bhutan has issued a number of bizarre postage stamps
made out of everything from silk to steel.

A false fact that's true.
The world's leading manufacturer and exporter of false teeth? The tiny mountainous European country of Liechtenstein.

The longest model railway in the world is in Germany. It spans nearly 10 miles.
That's railly crazy!

Planes are grounded.
The Brazilian capital of Brasilia was built from scratch in 1960. From the air, it **was designed to resemble an airplane**.

Energy boost!
Geothermal water is heated by underground volcanic activity. In Iceland, it's used as a power source. Geothermal heats nine out of 10 homes in the country.

A square deal?
The O'Connell Bridge in Dublin, Ireland, is the only bridge in Europe with a width that's nearly equal its length. It's 155 feet wide and 148 feet long.

Plenty of room!
There are an average of 4.7 people per square mile in the Asian country of Mongolia. **That makes Mongolia the least densely populated place on earth.**

There's a mailbox 33 feet underwater off the coast of Japan. Scuba divers use it to send postcards.
Wish you were here!

Every second, the equivalent of about 20,000 bathtubs full of water flow over Niagara Falls.
The water is a lot colder, however.

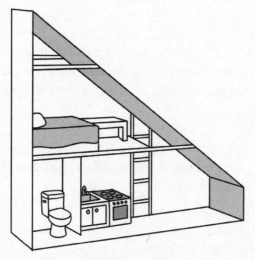

The Keret House in Warsaw, Poland, is just 28 inches wide—it's the world's thinnest house. Guess you don't need that panoramic setting to take a pic.

Louisiana is known for its swampy areas, called the wetlands.
They're larger than the entire state of Connecticut.
And wetter!

Niagara Falls isn't just one waterfall. It consists of three different falls: Horseshoe Falls, American Falls, and Bridal Veil Falls.
And we wouldn't want to dive into any of them!

If you're thirsty, just head north.
The largest amount of fresh water in the world sits in Canada. Its lakes and rivers contain 25 percent of the world's supply.

Hi, Bob!
In 1999, Canada's gigantic **Northwest Territories was almost renamed**. Residents voted to keep the name, but **one of the more popular choices floated was Bob.**

Yo, bro!
The Caribbean island of **Saint Barthélemy**, also known as St. Barts, **was originally named by explorers after Bartolomeo Columbus**.
He was Christopher Columbus's brother.

Some meaty facts: Canada is home to Sausage Lake, Tenderloin Mountain, and Pork Peninsula.

"Gotham" didn't originate with Batman comics. **The first Gotham City was a mythical town in England** where the residents were said to be very dumb. *Sounds like they could use the help of Batman!*

Oslo is the capital of Norway, but it wasn't always called that. Prior to 1925 it was called Christiania, after Norwegian king Christian IV. *(Or Chris for short.)*

How do you spell "Wisconsin"? Who knows? **The word Wisconsin residents look up how to spell the most often:** Wisconsin.

Sorry, H, you're fired. In the early 20th century, the government tried (and failed) to simplify the spelling of some words. As a result, **the city of Pittsburgh was briefly renamed Pittsburg.**

A whole language with half the letters! **There are only 13 letters in the traditional Hawaiian alphabet.** It uses eight consonants and five vowels.

It's not Paris! **Kinshasa is the capital of the Democratic Republic of the Congo** in Africa. **It's home to more French speakers** than any other city on the planet.

South Africa's nickname is the Rainbow Nation. It's a very diverse country—it has 11 official languages. *Word!*

Google Translate can't always help you.
About 5,000 languages are spoken on earth.
Some have only one or two speakers.

Same organization, different symbol:
In many Arab countries in the Middle East,
the Red Cross is known as the Red Crescent.

Happy Easter?
The name Spain comes from *Spania*.
It means "land of rabbits."

In Japan, they don't see a man in the moon.
In that country, it's called a "rabbit in the moon."
How bunny!

It's common in Brazil to take three or four showers a day. Guests are even offered a shower before a meal. Now that's really washing up before dinner!

What a capital idea!
The South American country of Bolivia has two capital cities. The court system is based in Sucre, while the rest of the government is located in La Paz.

The capital of the country of Syria is the oldest continually occupied capital city in the world. It was part of the Egyptian empire in 1500 B.C. *Lots of history there.*

Costa Rica doesn't have a military. Neither do 14 other countries. *Stay safe!*

Splat!
Tomatina is a festival held every year in Spain.
The main event: tomato throwing. Before the festival starts,
locals protect their homes with plastic sheeting.

Full steam ahead!
It's so cold in Finland that saunas (or steam baths)
are a part of the culture. Most people have one
installed in their homes, and 99 percent of the
population uses them on a regular basis.

Move your hands!
**In Indonesia it's considered rude to stand with your
hands on your hips.** People think it makes you seem greedy.

It's opposite land!
**In Bulgaria, Turkey, and Iran, shaking your head
side to side means yes.** Nodding up and down means no.

The world leader with the highest salary:
The Prime Minister of Singapore gets $1.7 million a year.
(The U.S. president gets just $400,000.)

Just a quick note:
The official currency of the U.S. is the U.S. dollar.
The U.S. dollar is also the official currency of
Ecuador, East Timor, El Salvador, Palau, Turks and Caicos,
the British Virgin Islands, and Zimbabwe.

Now that's golden!
**The official paint color of the Golden Gate Bridge
in San Francisco is orange, not gold.** The bridge is so
named because it runs over the Golden Gate Strait,
named by explorer John C. Frémont in 1846.

A good name for a huge mountain.
Mount Everest sits on the border of Nepal and Tibet.
**In the local Tibetan language, it's known as
Chomolungma,** or "goddess mother of the world."

You should have climbed it then.
**Mount Everest, the tallest mountain on the planet's
surface, is about a foot taller** today than it was
a century ago. It grows by about 4 millimeters a year.

Do not climb!
**The tallest unclimbed peak in the world
is Gangkhar Puensum in the Asian country of Bhutan.**
It's considered sacred by locals, and climbing above
6,000 meters is banned by the government.

This is earth-shaking!
In April 1868, a massive, 7.9-scale earthquake rocked Hawaii. Little earthquakes still happen in Hawaii, and scientists sa that they're actually **aftershocks from the great quake of '68.**

What a view!
Stand at the top of Mount Irazu in Costa Rica. **It's the only place where you can see the Atlantic Ocean and the Pacific Ocean at the same time**.

Let's turn things around.
In every country on earth, windmills turn counterclockwise. Except in Ireland—they turn clockwise there.

Standing tall! Stilts were invented by French shepherds. They needed a way to get around in wet marshes.

What's the word in French for "walkie-talkie"?
It's talkie-walkie.
Over!

Time for a pit stop.
In India, a gas station is called a "petrol bunk."
In Singapore, it's a "petrol kiosk." In Australia, it's a "servo."

They're in an Empire State of mind!
New York City is the most populous place
in the United States.
More people live in NYC than in 39 out of 50 U.S. states.

The last place on earth is Zywocice, Poland.
Well, alphabetically it is.

9
PLANES, TRAINS, AND AUTOMOBILES

This chapter is all about things that go: cars, jets, spaceships, and more. "Wheeeeeee" hope you like it!

In 1984, a man named Jack Smith traveled across the United States in 26 days. He did it on a skateboard. It's "ollie" ever wanted to do.

Taxi!
If you put them all together, **New York City cab drivers collectively drive one million miles a day.**

And we don't mean the chocolate kind. Moose roam onto roads in Sweden the way deer wander onto roads in many parts of the U.S. On an average day, 12 car accidents in Sweden happen when people swerve to avoid hitting moose.

Keep your eyes on the road.
In 2006, Dong Changsheng of China pulled a car 33 feet.
What's weird: He pulled it with his eyelids.

In Japan in 1990, the longest traffic jam of all time took place. It was 84 miles long.
It makes you wonder if there are still some people stuck!

No wonder it's so hard to find a parking space!
There are about a billion cars on the planet right now.
About a third of those are located in the United States.
The country with the second-most cars: China, with 78 million.

The first car race in America was held in Chicago in 1895. Cars sped at an average of . . . *whew!* . . . 7.5 miles per hour.

In Russia it's a criminal act to drive around in a car that's considered excessively dirty. Drawing "Wash me!" on a dirty car with your finger is basically calling the police.

The first cars in the late 1800s didn't have steering wheels.
People controlled the vehicle with a lever instead.
Is that what driving "stick" is all about?

The first automobile in history was built in 1668.
A Belgian priest working in China built a vehicle that was two feet long and powered by steam.
Now that's a compact car.

In case of zombie attack, consult your Hyundai.
In 2014, there was a "special edition" of the Hyundai Tucson available. **It came with a "Zombie Survival Kit."**

In Korean, the name of Korean car company **Hyundai means "modern."**
Well, this is the company that sold a car with an anti-zombie pack.

Flame on!
In South Africa, BMW drivers can opt to have a flamethrower installed. The car company says it can prevent carjackings.

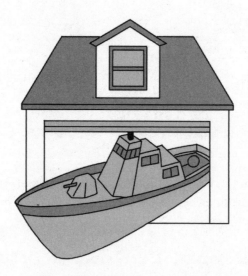

Corvette is the name of one of the most famous sports cars. It's also the name of a small warship. But you can only park one of them in the garage.

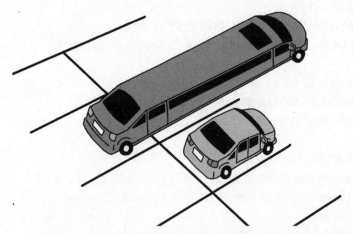

If your car were more than 42 feet long, what couldn't you do with it? Legally drive it on public roads in the United States. You also probably couldn't find a parking spot big enough.

Road trip!
The first coast-to-coast car trip took place in 1903.
From San Francisco to New York City, it took
63 days. (Cars and roads weren't as good back then.)

Where are my keys?!
What do 40 percent of car thefts have in common?
The owner left the keys in the ignition.

Gives new meaning to the phrase "a baby on the way."
Each year about 6,000 babies in the United States are born in a car or taxi on the way to the hospital.

Red all about it!
All car taillights are red, and they're all the exact same shade of red. Why? It's federal law.

It's red-hot . . .
The world's most popular car color: red.
Second-most popular: white.

We have you surrounded!
In 1899, police in Northamptonshire, England, borrowed a man's Benz car to chase down a man caught selling forged circus tickets.
It was the first-ever high-speed police chase . . .
although the car only went 12 miles per hour.

Ever see a strip or chunk of tire that's been left on the road? The truck driver slang term for that is a "road alligator." See you later, alligator.

Why the long face?
The first police car owned and operated by a police department was put into use in 1903. The Boston Police Department used a car called a Stanley Steamer that put four horses out of work.

Henry Ford, chairman of the Ford Motor Company who helped popularize cars in the United States, **gave his son Edsel a car.** He was eight years old at the time, and **he drove himself to school in it.** *Guess he didn't have to wait for his sweet 16.*

Edsel didn't have a license, but that runs in the family. **Henry Ford never actually had a driver's license.**

Soy what? Henry Ford was "green" before it was cool. **In 1941, Ford made a car—and everything in it—completely out of soybeans.**

The Philion Road Carriage was patented in 1892. It could reach a top speed of eight miles per hour, and you could place the steering wheel in either the front or the back of the car. *True backseat driving.*

Where did they proclaim love for pets and vacation spots?
Before 1927, there were no bumper stickers, because there were no bumpers on cars! When bumpers were introduced as a safety feature, people began to attach flaglike signs to cars with wires or string. Actual stickers came in the 1940s.

Good news!
General Motors demonstrated the first-ever solar car in 1955. *Bad news!* It was only 15 inches long, and way too small to drive.

Who wants a gas-sicle?
According to the experts, a car will get slightly better gas mileage if the gasoline put into it is very cold.

In 1966, the **National Safety Council recognized a famous person for promoting proper seat belt use.** That person: Batman.
What about Robin?

Today's cars have rear-facing cameras to show drivers what they're backing up into, but **a camera was an option on cars as early as 1919.** The Templar Motor Company's **1919 Roadster could be outfitted with a camera mounted on the hood.**
Want the high-tech package? They came with compasses as well.

Car historians consider 1886 the birth of the automotive age. That year, German inventor Carl Benz built a vehicle called the Benz Patent-Motorwagen.
Wouldn't you name it after yourself?

People started using cars regularly in the mid-1880s. **The first used car lot was invented in 1897.** They had 17 cars for sale.
And probably a lot of great deals.

Until 1923, **drivers in Italy drove on the right side in the country, and on the left side in the city.**
The day they switched it over must have been chaotic.

How very crafty!
License plates weren't always made of metal. They were once made of everything from porcelain to cardboard to leather.

New Hampshire's license plate slogan is "Live free or die."
Inmates of the state prison make those license plates.
How ironic.

You can copyright a color?
Trucks from UPS (the United Parcel Service) are brown.
**They're a very specific shade called Pullman Brown,
which UPS trademarked.** Nobody else can use it.

Here's another one coming off the line.
About 165,000 cars are produced in factories
around the world **every day.**

Since the year 1970, the number of cars being made
each year has doubled. **But world bicycle production
has quadrupled!**
It's really switched into high gear!

**In Brazil, more than 90 percent of all new cars
run on ethanol fuel.** It's made out of sugar cane.
How sweet it is!

For here or to go?
Everybody has a meal on the go, or hits the drive-through
once in a while. **Americans eat an average of one out
of every five meals in the car.**

Start your "engines."
Modern cars, especially hybrid cars, use a lot of
sophisticated technology and don't make
a lot of noise. **Many car engine sounds are faked,
piped through tiny speakers in the car.**

Electric cars are nothing new. They were manufactured by a company called Rauch & Lang from 1905 to 1920. *And then somebody got gas.*

Don't just sit there on the sofa–do something! In 2011, a guy named Glenn Suter outfitted his couch with a motorcycle engine. Then he rode it at 101 miles per hour, a land speed record for couches.

Time for a name change?
The Volkswagen Beetle (or "Bug") is one of the most popular cars of all time. **When it was first made in Germany in 1945, the VW Beetle was called Kraft durch Freude Wage,** or "Strength Through Joy Car."

Mary Anderson invented windshield wipers in 1902.
Car companies didn't want them at first because they said they'd distract drivers.
Well, sure, but you can turn them off if it's not raining!

So many vehicles boast of their speed and power by listing "horsepower." **What exactly is horsepower?** One unit of horsepower is the amount of force it takes to lift 550 pounds for one foot for one second. *Guess that does seem like a feat to brag about.*

The first Harley Davidson motorcycle was built in 1903. One of its parts was a used, empty tomato can. *Try to ketchup!*

The most-produced motor vehicle in world history is the Honda Super Club motorcycle. Since 1958, more than 100 million of them have been made. *That's a lot of members in the Club!*

Motorcycles were practical before cars were. Steam-powered mechanical bicycles were demonstrated in Paris in 1818, about 70 years before cars took off in popularity. *Vroom-vroom!*

Silence!
What are ray guns, drag pipes, and peashooters? Nicknames motorcycle riders have given to mufflers.

It was a cold and lonely right.
Why is Fukashi Kazami in the record books? In 1987, **he became the first person to ride a motorcycle all the way to the North Pole.**

Better to only ride Formula Rossa on a sunny day!
Experts say that a roller coaster travels an average
of 10 miles per hour faster if it's raining.

This story could get bumpy.
Those raised-bump reflectors on roads have a name.
They're called Botts' Dots, after their inventor, Elbert Botts.

It just keeps chugging along.
**The longest railway in the world is Russia's
Trans-Siberian Railway.** It's almost 6,000 miles long.

Hope you're strapped in tightly.
Formula Rossa is a roller coaster at the Ferrari World
theme park in Abu Dhabi. **It goes about as fast as
a Ferrari—149 miles per hour.**

Progress is in the air!
In 1903, Orville and Wilbur Wright completed the first successful flight of an airplane: It lasted 59 seconds. Just 66 years later, the first man walked on the moon.

Two years before that first plane flight, **Wilbur Wright reportedly told a friend that "man won't fly for 50 years."** *He proved himself wrong!*

A hop, skip, and a wing . . .
The wingspan of a Boeing 747 is 195 feet. That's more than the length of the Wright Brothers' first flight back in 1903.

Airplane parts are very expensive. **The windshield of a Boeing 747 costs about the same as a luxury car.** *But a luxury car can't fly!*

Just plane smart:
If a commercial airplane pilot gets sick, the copilot can take over. That's why **they never eat the same in-flight meal—** so they don't both get food poisoning.

If you've ever been in a busy airport, it doesn't feel that way. Only **5 percent of the entire population** of the world **has ever ridden in an airplane.**

Thousands of flights take place every day. **It's estimated that at any given time, three million people are up in the air.** *Hello, up there!*

There are many women in the profession now, but when air travel began in the 1910s, **the first flight attendants were men**. First one: German man Heinrich Kubis in 1912. *How do you say, "Can I have a ginger ale?" in German?*

First American female pilot: Harriet Quimby. She got her pilot's license in 1911, and became the first woman to fly over the English Channel in 1912. *She soared above the competition.*

Hey, you know this one.
The international language of flight is English.
All pilots and air traffic controllers are required to speak it.

President of the sky!
The president of the United States has a private plane, but it's not necessarily Air Force One. **Air Force One is the air traffic call signal for any plane on which the president is aboard.**

Brace for landing:
Airport runways are about four feet thick.
All those layers of asphalt absorb impact.

The largest jet in the world is the Antonov AN-225.
This cargo jet is about the size of a football field.
Hike!

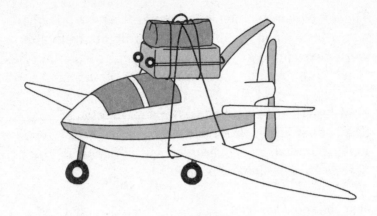

The smallest jet in the world is the BD-5 Micro. It seats one, has a wingspan of about 20 feet, and weighs 358 pounds. Sorry, no room for your luggage.

It's a gas!
Airplanes require a tremendous amount of fuel. **A Boeing 767-400 uses the same amount of gas that would fill up the tanks of 1,400 minivans.**

A lot of ups and downs . . .
The world's shortest regularly scheduled airline flight: between the Scottish highlands of Westray and Papa Westray. **The 1.5 mile flight takes just two minutes.**

Are we there yet?
In 1986, a plane called *Voyager* flew completely around the world. It was a nonstop flight—without refueling.

The first successful helicopter flight happened in 1907. It lasted for 20 seconds and the vehicle lifted a foot off the ground.
So it was a little choppy.

ZAP!
Airplanes are designed to withstand lightning strikes.
They do it all the time.

The longest ship in the world is the Prelude FNG, a South Korean vessel. At 1,601 feet, it's longer than the Empire State Building would be if you laid it on its side. *But please don't do that.*

Oar maybe you already knew this fact?
What's it called when you propel a boat with oars? Sculling.

Hello down there

Big words: Skywriters can write a message in exhaust in the sky. So it can be seen from the ground, the average letter is about two miles high.

If you set sail from the latitude of 60° south, **it's possible to sail around the world without ever reaching land.**
Every rest stop has a pool!

The first ship to pass through the Panama Canal in 1914 was the *S.S. Ancorn*. It was carrying a load of cement.
Must have been a hard journey.

There's no secret code here.
Think S.O.S. stands for "Save Our Ship"? It doesn't really mean anything. It was chosen as a distress signal because it's easy to transmit in Morse code: three dots, three dashes, three dots.

Don't get steamed about how simple this one is.
What does the "S.S." in a ship's name stand for?
Steamship.

Time to hit the gas station again.
Aircraft carriers don't run on regular gasoline—
most are nuclear powered. If they did run on gasoline,
they'd get six inches to the gallon.

**Over a period of 200 years, three ships crashed in
the same place off the coast of Wales**—all on
December 5. All had one survivor, and in all three
shipwrecks, the survivor was named Hugh Williams.
Now that's just spooky.

Why are big boats called yachts? It's from the Dutch
word *yacht,* which means hunt. Dutch sailors once used
large boats to "hunt" down pirates.
Arrrrrgh!

Aliens?
In August 1783, **Jacques Charles launched the first
unmanned hydrogen balloon.** It floated into
a village in France, where the people freaked out and
destroyed the balloon with pitchforks.

Why buy when you could rent?
In ancient Roman times, there were businesses where
people could pay to rent a chariot for the day.

In 1982, a California man named Larry Walters tied 45
weather balloons to a lawn chair. It propelled him
to 16,000 feet in the air, and after 45 minutes airborne
he used a pellet gun to pop the balloons and safely
land below. Hey, it's just like *Up!*

It takes the International Space Station just 0.2 seconds to travel one mile. *It's the cheetah of space!*

Blast off!
How fast does a rocket have to go to escape the Earth's gravity? Seven miles . . . per second.

10
ODDBALLS

We salute these facts that are totally weird and random
and don't quite fit in anywhere else. (We can relate!)

Everything has a musical pitch to it. Most toilets flush
in the key of E flat. Is it music to your ears?

Flushed away!
In 2014, **38 million gallons of water had to
be drained from a reservoir in Portland.** Why?
Somebody went to the bathroom in it!

Right now there are about $40 billion worth of American coins in circulation. Start searching the sofa to collect 'em all!

It pays to save!
The average home has about six pounds of pennies in it. That's not even counting all the dimes, nickels, and quarters.

It's 50-50 odds whether a coin lands on "heads" or "tails," right? Not always. **A penny is more likely to land on heads,** because Lincoln's face weighs more than the Lincoln Memorial on the back.
So maybe call "heads" the next time you have to do a coin toss.

Worth it?
How much does it cost to mint a nickel?
About 10 cents.

Reed all about it!
**A dime has exactly 118 ridges
around its edge.** They're called "reeds."

Big money.
In 2007 Canada issued a $1 million coin.
It weighed 220 pounds and was made of solid gold.

There is an estimated $44 billion worth
of unused gift cards floating around out there.
More sofa searching?

Half of all bank robberies take place on Friday.
Talk about payday.

U.S. money isn't made from paper. It's made from a blend of cotton and linen.
Which is why a bill doesn't get destroyed in the wash when you leave it in your pocket.

Here's a gore-y fact:
The part of a sock where the toes go is called the "toe," **but the heel has a name, too:** the gore.

We found the one good thing about Mondays!
It's the only day of the week that has a one-word anagram. It's "dynamo."

The average office worker types on a computer keyboard an average **of 90,000 keystrokes a day.**
That's a lot of clickety-clacks!

(Laser) tag, you're it!
The beam in a laser pointer is a low-powered beam of pure light. It could **potentially be seen up to a quarter of a mile away.**

Leather shoes tend to squeak. Athletic shoes don't—which is why they are also called *sneakers*. As quiet as a mouse!

The tallest volcano on Mars is called Olympus Mons.
It's about 16 miles tall, about four times as tall as Earth's tallest volcano, South America's Ojos del Salado.
It's "only" four miles tall.

The thing that writes in a pencil isn't lead—it's graphite. But there's enough of it in a single pencil to draw a line that's 38 miles long. And you can always erase it if you make a mistake.

TV satellites orbit around the Earth very high in the sky. They operate best at about 22,300 miles above the surface. So then all TV comes...from space?

Waving the white flag.
In 1969, **astronauts left an American flag on the moon**. Scientists say that space radiation **has probably bleached it by now**.

It's not as hot as it could be.
The sun's atmosphere stretches millions of miles into space, past the Earth. **That means that, technically, we live on the sun!**

The sun is bigger than the Earth, but how much bigger? **About a million times bigger.**
Give or take.

Venus rotates in the opposite direction than Earth does, which means sunrises and sunsets work the opposite way there. The sun rises in the west, and it sets in the east.

Only two planets in the solar system don't have any moons: Mercury and Venus. Guess you can't blame crazy behavior on a full moon there.

Things are heating up!
Today, the sun is 30 percent hotter than it was 4.6 billion years ago. (That's when the solar system formed.)

A summer on the planet Uranus lasts more than 20 years.
But hey, so does a winter!

Wake up!
In space no one can hear you snore. That's because **it's impossible to snore in the weightlessness of space.**

But weight!
The earth weighs more every year.
It's put on about 100,000 tons since last year.

The word *astronaut* comes from two Greek words put together. It literally translates to "star sailor." Come sail away!

Best to just stay on the edges:
There's a black hole in the center of the
Milky Way galaxy, and it's 14 million miles wide.

Up, up, and away!
They look so fluffy, but they're not.
The average cloud weighs more than a million pounds.

If you were able to locate and then cut into **a large enough hailstone, you'd see that it's made up of rings,** just like an onion.
But it won't make your eyes tear up.

How are bolts of lightning like fingerprints?
No two are identical.
They're one of a kind!

Park ranger Roy Sullivan appeared in Guinness World Records **for being struck by lightning more** times than any other person: seven.
We're shocked . . . but not as much as poor Roy.

Air it is!
Snow is only about 10 percent water.
Which means it's about 90 percent air.

All that heat must pack a punch.
Hot water is slightly heavier than cold water.

Ice isn't actually slippery. When pressure is applied to it, a very thin layer melts into cold water.
And that's what is slippery.

Only in the movies...
The chances of sinking in quicksand are slim.
Most quicksand is just a few inches deep.

Outta my way!
At room temperature, an air molecule runs into
a billion other air molecules every second.

True or false: **Mythomaniacs are people who can't stop lying**.
It's true!

You've "almost" got it!
What's the longest word in the English language with all of the letters in alphabetical order? It's *almost*.

3,000,000,000,000,00
0,000,000,000,000,00
0,000,000,000

What's a duodecillion?
It's a number: 1 followed by 39 zeroes.
Start counting...

There are a lot of ups and downs.
Research shows that people start to get restless and fidgety if an elevator doesn't come within 40 seconds.

Where did the time go?
Experts say we spend about one year of our lives **looking for lost objects**.

Ahhhh! Tests!
Do you have scholionophobia?
That's the technical name for "fear of school."

Feel it!
What's the longest word in the English language that doesn't have a vowel? Rhythm.

We thought we dreamt this up.
There's only one word in English that ends with "mt."
It's "dreamt."

#Trivia.
The "hash" symbol in hashtags has a name.
It's an octotroph.

To lemniscate and beyond!
That curvy infinity sign also has a name.
It's called a lemniscate.

A common diagnosis:
A song that gets stuck in your head is called an earworm. Researchers say at least 90 percent of people get a tune stuck in their head once a week.

Singing is good for you. Taking the mic for one song burns about two calories. Sing your heart out!

Here's a tittle fact . . .
The dot over the letters "i" and "j" is called a tittle.

It's not just orange.
There are a handful of words in English that don't rhyme with anything: orange (of course), purple, silver, and month.

XYZ or YKK?
The YKK on your zipper stands for Yoshida Kogyo Kabushikigaisha. The YKK Group is a Japanese group of manufacturing companies and the world's largest zipper manufacturer.

In 1797, James Hetherington invented the top hat. When he wore it in public, he was arrested for causing a scene. Hats off!

Shiny and similar.
Sapphires are blue and rubies are red.
That's the only difference between those
precious gems—**chemically, they're identical.**

Why are schoolhouses traditionally painted red?
In the 1800s, that was the cheapest paint color.
Nobody would trust a polka-dotted school anyway.

A fact that might float your boat:
In the past, **life jackets were filled with sunflower stems.**
Before plastic foam came along, cork, balsa wood,
and kapok (material from a tropical tree) were also used.

The newest letter in the English alphabet is J.
It wasn't adopted until the 1600s.
If there was no J, would be a PB&J just be a PB?

Does the "O" stand for "Old?"
The oldest letter in our alphabet is O.
It dates back to 3000 B.C.

Stand still and look closely.
**The "Don't" in the "Don't Walk" sign
is misspelled**—the apostrophe is missing.

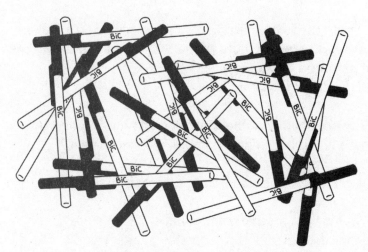

Since 1950, Bic has sold an average of
50 ballpoint pens a second.
That's a lot of writing!

Hello, technical support?
How many photocopier accidents are caused by people sitting on them to make a "copy" of their rear end? About 25 percent.

Think twice before you hit print!
Which costs more: printer ink or gasoline? On a gallon-by-gallon basis, the ink costs 1,400 times more than gas.

Say selfie!
Every two minutes, we take more pictures than all of humanity did in the 19th century.

A smartphone is a miracle of modern science. **To make one work requires more than 250,000 individual pieces of patented technology**.
All that to make Twitter work!

Why are phone numbers seven digits long? Because that's about the longest number people can easily memorize.
But then area codes came along to mess it up.

What is "percussive maintenance"? That's the technical term for hitting something until it works.
Then you have to try turning it off and back on again.

Bored? Pop the walls of your room!
Engineers Alfred Fielding and Marc Chavannes were actually
working on a **new type of textured wallpaper when they
came up with bubble wrap** in 1957.

But make it snappy.
Want to make rubber bands last longer?
Stick them in the refrigerator.

Do you have a moment?
**In medieval times a "moment" was a measure
of time equal to about 90 seconds.**
Thank you for your time.

You can read this in a jiffy!
A "jiffy" is also an actual, measurable unit of time.
It's one 100th of a second.

Think you can remember this? *Lethologica* **is the inability
to remember a particular word.**
Like, say, lethologica.

**The most common street name in the U.S. isn't
First Street.** It's Second Street.
Huh?

Worms, bears, and gas!
No matter how cold it gets, gasoline won't freeze.
When the temperature drops below minus 180°F, it just
turns gummy.

Oil is nicknamed "black gold." It can also be
red, brown, or green.
But it's always sticky.

That's a big bunny!
All of the dust in your house really adds up.
One home gathers about 40 pounds of dust every year.

Thirsty?
If you poured all the oceans of the world into glasses
of water, **there would still be fewer total glasses than
there are atoms in just one of those glasses of water.**

He was hoping for a cure but not holding his breath.
Charles Osborne, of Iowa, holds the record for the
longest attack of hiccups—68 years, from 1922 to 1990.
Total estimated hiccups: 430 million.

The largest working yo-yo ever made was more than 10 feet tall and weighed almost 900 pounds. That's about the size of a polar bear. A polar bear can't do as many tricks, though.

What a burn!
Here's how those trick birthday candles work.
The wick contains a small amount of magnesium.
When it gets lit and someone tries to blow it out,
everything but the magnesium stops burning . . . and
a few seconds later the magnesium ignites it all again.

Rock, paper, diamond . . .
The only thing that can scratch a diamond is a diamond.

Since **Silly Putty was invented in 1950, 300 million
plastic eggs of the stuff** have been sold. That's enough
to make a ball the size of a blimp.
How silly!

There are 12 gardeners on staff at the Mirage Hotel in Las Vegas. **Their job: attend to artificial plants.**
Hope they don't remember to water the plants.

Thou shalt not steal!
The Bible is the **most shoplifted book in the United States**.

Does this bug you?
When early computer programmer Grace Hopper was working one day, **a moth flew into the machine and shorted it out. That's why a computer error is called a "bug."**

In 2013, **the Hornsleth Deep Storage Project lowered an iron sculpture into a trench in the ocean. It's full of human blood**, hair samples, and animal DNA. It's there to bring people or animals back to life in the future.
It's good to have a backup plan.

"Never odd or even" spelled backward is still "Never odd or even."
Always odd!

Stretched out, a Slinky will reach out from a sixth-story window all the way down to the ground. But don't do that, because you can't get it back into shape.